THE ART & CRAFT OF
CERAMICS

Maria Dolors Ros i Frigola

THE ART & CRAFT OF
CERAMICS

LARK
BOOKS

Ros i Frigola, Maria Dolors, 1947-
    The art & craft of ceramics : techniques, projects, inspiration / Maria Dolors Ros i Frigola.
        p. cm.
    Includes bibliographical references and index.
    ISBN 1-57990-912-4 (hardcover)
    1. Pottery craft. I. Title. II. Title: Art and craft of ceramics.
TT920.R683 2006
738—dc22   2006012613

10 9 8 7 6 5 4 3 2 1

Published in the United States by:
Lark Books, 67 Broadway, Asheville, NC 28801
www.larkbooks.com

First printing: May 2006

English translation © Lark Books, 2006

Distributed in Canada by Sterling Publishing, c/o Canadian Manda Group,
165 Dufferin Street Toronto, Ontario, Canada M6K 3H6

The Art & Craft of Ceramics

Project and Production
Parramón Ediciones, S.A.

Text:
Maria Dolors Ros i Frigola

Project Demonstrations:
Barbaformosa, Ivet Bazaco, Carlets, Josep Matés, Yukiko Murata

Collection Design:
Josep Guasch

Photography:
Nos & Soto i Maria Dolors Ros

Illustrations:
Estudi Farrés

Layout:
Estudi Guasch, Inc.

Translated from Spanish by
Eric A. Bye, M.A.

First Edition: September 2005

© Parramón Ediciones, S.A.
Exclusive publishing rights worldwide.

5 Ronda de Sant Pere, 4th floor
08010 Barcelona, Spain
www.parramon.com

A Subsidiary of Norma Publishing Group

© Marc Chagall, Georges Braque, Madola, Rosa Amorós, VEGAP, Barcelona 2005
© Pablo Picasso Estate. VEGAP, Barcelona, 2005
© The Isamu Noguchi Foundation and Garden Museum / VEGAP, Barcelona

Pre-printing: Pacmer, Inc.

Printed in Spain

Cont

ents

Introduction

First of all, I must confess that I found it difficult to condense all the techniques addressed into just a few pages. Some subjects deserved more space. However, in the limited space available, I think I have succeeded in providing a glimpse into ceramics, from starting the process to further exploring some of the more complex subjects.

I would like to remind the reader that it will not be easy to achieve a level of professionalism by merely reading this book. You have to practice over and over again, with patience; in this art form, time is on the artist's side. When something turns out badly, you must try again. Never be satisfied, and never get discouraged.

Even after 50 years of working, a ceramist can make new and interesting discoveries and produce results never before imagined. The art of ceramics is in large part a direct, continuous experience of an individual's discoveries throughout the years. This book is intended to be a modest orientation, an invitation, and a brief introduction to the most important technical principles. After a few years of working with clay, every one of you will be able to write your own book, filled with new experiences that are useful to you and to others. My greatest wish will be granted if reading this book instills in young artists a spirit of perseverance and a passion for ceramics.

In addition, it would be very rewarding if a reader who uses this initial advice discovers new methods and techniques in the future. In such a case, these pages will have achieved one of my goals: to motivate, stimulate, promote, and encourage interested readers to experience the great satisfactions—and the frustrations—of working with clay.

In this illustrated book, I have introduced basic and more technical aspects of ceramics and have arranged them in order of increasing difficulty, which is the way I believe learning should proceed.

The first chapter is an overview of contemporary ceramics of the 20th century. I have mentioned only the most representative artists; I've surely left out some distinguished names.

I would like to express my appreciation for the tremendous work done by so many ceramists in their tireless struggle to ensure the survival of contemporary ceramics.

The second chapter deals with everything related to raw materials, their preparation, and their use. This is one of the most important aspects of getting started. If artists aren't familiar with the materials used to create clay objects, they will experience a number of problems.

The third chapter explains the various tools and equipment used in working with clay. This same chapter also includes descriptions of the most essential firing techniques, as well as advice on working with kilns and their various atmospheres.

The fourth chapter covers some of the most important and basic production methods in such a way that someone who has little experience in the field of ceramics can understand the material. There is also an introduction to the potter's wheel and the possibilities it offers.

It was not easy to explain the chemical principles of complex glaze technology in a concise, practical way. I have synthesized the most basic aspects so the reader can see how they function. If there is further interest, the beginning potter can experiment in his or her own studio. In this same chapter, I have explained—in a simple manner—some interesting materials and methods, such as copper reds, ash glazes, paper clay, and raku, to demonstrate that ceramics has no limits.

Six step-by-step projects are illustrated; they are specific and exhaustive in showing how different artists work. I'm sure you will learn something from every one of them and continue to learn as you work, as the act of learning should be a constant in our lives.

Finally, the Gallery depicts work that illustrates the latest artistic techniques. The artists are some of the most renowned of our time. Unfortunately, I have not been able to include many others due to space limitations.

I wish to conclude this introduction by thanking the readers for their confidence in choosing this book. I hope something is learned from these pages about the world of ceramics, which has helped me so greatly in understanding the human and artistic philosophy of life.

Maria Dolors Ros i Frigola (Serra de Daró, 1947) is a ceramist who combines her creativity as an artist with an intense devotion to teaching ceramics. A graduate in applied arts with a major in ceramics from the Escola Massana in Barcelona, she has developed her own teaching style over the years. She has organized numerous summer courses since 1972 and has taught ceramics in many schools and institutions in Spain, as well as in schools throughout Central America.

In 1992, with aid from the Generalitat de Catalunya, she helped establish a center for Applied Arts: the Ceramics School at La Bisbal, which she has directed since its founding. Devoted to raising the level of ceramics instruction, she has also organized clay classes for both public and private institutions. In addition, she has received a European master's degree in sculptural ceramics and has worked with ceramists in her region to improve their businesses. She is currently developing a ceramics-focused library in Forallac (Girona, Spain), which, along with La Bisbal, is a city well known for ceramics production.

During the Neolithic Age, humans ceased being hunters and wanderers, and settled in areas where they could work the land and raise animals. They organized their social structure based on agriculture and livestock; as a result, it became necessary to store foods. When they discovered that fire changed clay into a stable material, ceramic vessels became essential items. Some of the oldest known pieces date from around 6000 B.C., and come from Anatolia, Syria, and Asia Minor, but it took until the end of the following millennium for ceramics to spread over the Mediterranean Sea throughout all of Europe and Egypt. Starting around 3000 B.C., ceramics appeared in the Far East, and the Minoan ceramics of Crete gained importance and spread as far as the Iberian Peninsula. The first vessels were made by pinching. The invention of the potter's wheel was the first major change in the evolution of ceramics. In addition to being practical, ceramics throughout history have become objects of ornamentation and art. In these few pages, we will not deal with this evolution over the course of centuries, since that would too vast a topic—enough for a separate book. Here, we merely intend to provide an overview of the development of ceramics in the last century, which surely was one of the most creative ones, to give the reader a basic idea of the rich panorama of modern ceramic art.

Contemporary Ceramics

The Evolution of Ceramics in the 20th Century

After the Industrial Revolution, ceramics were mass-produced and lost all artistic value until the Arts and Crafts Movement began in London in 1888. William Morris and John Ruskin proposed a complete reform of the arts in favor of hand-crafted pieces; they sought the purest beauty in objects for daily use and rejected technology and new materials. This concept cultivated a taste for hand-made items, and the applied arts once again came to be highly regarded.

At the same time, world's fairs and expositions at the end of the 19th century increased awareness in Europe about ceramics from China and Japan, which became two of the most important areas for ceramics production. Their aesthetic and technical quality reestablished the artistic merit of ceramics, took it out of factories, and returned it to craft workshops.

Creativity in the First Decades of the 20th Century

The 20th century also saw the emergence of Art Nouveau, an artistic movement that spread throughout Europe and adapted the philosophy of the Arts and Crafts Movement to the reality of the times. Based on the union of industry and art to create a useful and beautiful product, this movement solidified the basis for design and allowed art and craft to gain ground so that functional items became luxury products, and people began to see ceramics as an art form.

The aesthetic of Modernism stressed the influence of Asian art, which made use of natural shapes for decorative and linear motifs, thus anticipating the abstract shapes that would later govern the Bauhaus School, begun in Weimar, Germany, in 1919.

In the early European vanguard of the 20th century, painters such as Marquet, Duffy, Braque, and Gauguin were attracted to Asian ceramics and the sculptural novelty that this material made possible. Later on, Chagall, Léger, Matisse, Kandinsky, Malèvich, and Rodin also decorated some ceramic work.

▶ Marc Chagall, *David and Bathsheba in the Moonlight*, 1952 Height 18 inches (46 cm). White clay

▶ Paul Gauguin, *Oviri*, 1895. 29 inches (74 cm). Glazed stoneware

▲ Georges Braque, *Mandolin*, 1945. Diameter 10 inches (25.5 cm)

The introduction of these artists to the world of ceramics and the functionalist aesthetic of the Bauhaus blurred the boundaries between the various artistic disciplines. At the same time, such ceramists as Bernard Leach and Shoji Hamada were investigating new ways to express a very personal language—creating studio ceramics—a concept that, pursued by such artists as Michael Cardew, Lucie Rie, and Hans Coper in Europe, and Peter Voulkos and Daniel Rhodes in the United States, was to change ceramics on a global level.

In addition, Isamu Noguchi became an important figure in bridging the gulf between the United States and Japan. Born in the United States and later influenced by Constantin Brancusi, Noguchi established a foundation for ceramic sculpture in Japan, where Kimie Sato, Yukio Yoshikawa, and many others have worked. Today, Yuhki Tanaka is a Japanese ceramist who works on an international level.

Ceramics after World War II

It's important to note that shortly after the war, Pablo Picasso and Joan Miró adopted the language of fire, which contributed more to the general rise of ceramics than to their individual artistic evolution. Picasso poured himself into research and experimentation; allowed himself to follow his instincts; and modified, transformed, and juxtaposed thrown pieces, which had started out as traditional forms.

The ceramics of Miró were completely linked to that of his friend, ceramist Josep Llorens Artigas. His relationship with surrealism and a desire to surpass the limits of painting led the painter to the world of the three-dimensional. Llorens Artigas left behind the classicism and serenity of his shapes to enter into the fantastic, rash world of Miró.

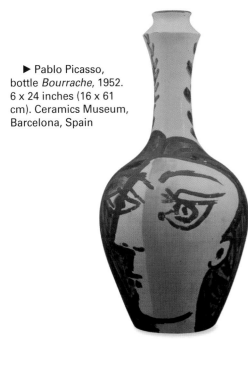

▶ Pablo Picasso, bottle *Bourrache*, 1952. 6 x 24 inches (16 x 61 cm). Ceramics Museum, Barcelona, Spain

▲ Pablo Picasso, *Zoomorphic Pitcher*, 1954. 14 x 7 x 12 inches (35 x 17 x 30 cm). Ceramics Museum, Barcelona, Spain

▶ Isamu Noguchi, *Karatsu kakutsubo*, 1952. Height 89 inches (226 cm). Stoneware

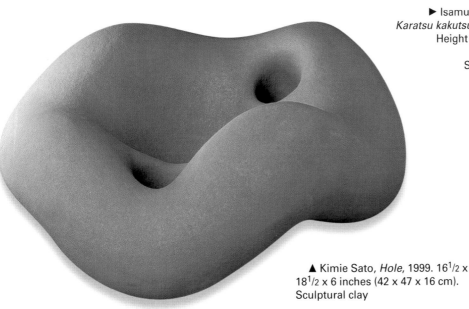

▲ Kimie Sato, *Hole*, 1999. 16^1/$_2$ x 18^1/$_2$ x 6 inches (42 x 47 x 16 cm). Sculptural clay

The two artists brought to ceramics a new concept that was essential to its renewal: freedom. They broke down the barriers of thrown ceramics and demonstrated that it could express a range of emotions, just like any other art form. Among the European ceramists who were devoted to ceramics as an art form, there were two geniuses in Spain who stood out: Llorens Artigas and Antoni Cumella. The contributions of the former to European ceramics in the 20th century were crucial, for he renewed the art form, creating an alternative to Asian ceramics. If the decorative concept of ceramics changed with Llorens Artigas, it was Cumella who came to question the shapes of these pieces. Later, artists such as Arcadio Blasco, Enric Mestre, Claudi Casanovas, and many others gained distinction by transforming the panorama of Spanish ceramics.

The Second World War forced many European ceramists to immigrate to the United States, and that phenomenon blurred territorial boundaries and encouraged artistic exchange between the two continents. In the midst of the political and social instability of that period, the provocative intent of artistic activity also affected ceramics. The ties established between the United States and Europe allowed the ceramists of the 20th century to search for identity and freedom—characteristics of contemporary art.

There was an anthropocentric language in which artists left their marks: American Abstract Expressionism. Through painting, it alluded to the sensations and emotions of the

▲ Peter Voulkos, *Dropout*, 1990

▲ Josep Llorens Artigas and Joan Miró. Detail of the monumental mural at Barcelona Airport, 1970

◀ Enric Mestre, Untitled, 1993. 19 x 13 x 12 inches (48 x 34 x 30 cm). Glazed stoneware and silicon carbide

▶ Arcadio Blasco, Ceramic mural. 27^1/$_2$ x 31^1/$_2$ inches (70 x 80 cm). Sculptural clay

artist. One of the best known of these artists was Jackson Pollock, who conceived of pictorial creation as a true ritual. Action painting arose from the fact that the artist literally became integrated into his work by giving free rein to his state of mind. Expressions, improvisation, and chance are some of the traits of this art form, which, when translated to the world of ceramics, made it possible to rediscover ancient techniques such as Japanese raku, whose main proponent was Paul Soldner.

American Abstract Expressionism guided ceramics through a fairly experimental terrain, thanks to the revolutionary contributions of Peter Voulkos. Influenced by European art, he became a leader in avant-garde ceramics and opened up many avenues that several generations of ceramists have continued to explore, including Paul Soldner, John Mason, Robert Arneson, Ken Price, and Bodil Manz.

◀ Bodil Manz, *Displaced Oval Form*, 2000. Porcelain with black bands

▼ Bernard Leach, Stoneware jug with temmoku glaze

◀ Antoni Cumella, Glazed stoneware mural. 26 x 19 inches (67 x 48 cm)

◀ Peter Voulkos, Untitled, 1989.

▶ Collaboration by Joan Miró and Josep Llorens Artigas. Terra cotta fired at low temperature

Within the American setting, we mustn't overlook the Archie Bray Foundation for the Ceramic Arts (established in Montana in 1951), where renowned artists Rudy Autio and Peter Voulkos met Bernard Leach and Shoji Hamada to expand the realities of ceramics.

Around 1960 in Europe, specifically in the United Kingdom, the Leach tradition was in the hands of Alan Caiger-Smith and Michael Casson, among others. They both sought their own identity, however, through techniques as divergent as lusters and salt glazes, respectively. Tony Hepburn and Richard Slee took things further and in very different ways progressed toward a combination of ceramics with other artistic and industrial techniques. Working with new technologies expanded the range of possibilities and provided greater freedom of expression, which continually brought ceramics into the present moment. Again in the United Kingdom, the work of Ewen Henderson, Martin Smith, and Elizabeth Fritsch is also significant.

The ceramic work of the Italian-Argentinian ceramist Lucio Fontana is a solid point of reference for such artists as Nino Caruso, Pompeo Pianezzola, and Carlo Zauli. These Italian ceramists distanced themselves from the ceramics of Faenza.

▲ Rudy Autio, *White Hall Vessel*, 1987. 30 x 21 x 22 inches (76 x 53 x 56 cm). Stoneware

► Martin Smith, *Vessel*. 8 x 11 x 5³/₄ inches (21 x 29 x 14.5 cm). Red clay, epoxy, and copper leaf

▼ Tony Hepburn, *Draw Shave*, 1992.

▲ Richard Slee, *Trowel*. 16¹/₂ inches (42 cm). Earthenware

In France, in addition to the movements developing in Paris, where the limits of art were constantly being questioned and ceramics was slowly making its way into the avant-garde realm, it's important to mention the work of the ceramists of La Borne. They have always strived for a personal style in ceramics, but their work slowly took on a more sculptural quality, in contrast to the mass production of the factories in Limoges and Sèvres. The works of J. Steadman, I. Mohy, and E. Joulia are particularly noteworthy.

In Germany, Michael Cleff and Ruth Duckworth were among the artists who were incorporating ceramics into their sculpture. There were also a number of collaborations involving the ceramist Hans Spinner and such artists as Anthony Caro, James Brown, and J. Plemsa. It was also thanks to Spinner that Antoni Tàpies used clay to give expression to his creative language and that Eduardo Chillida challenged solid sculpture.

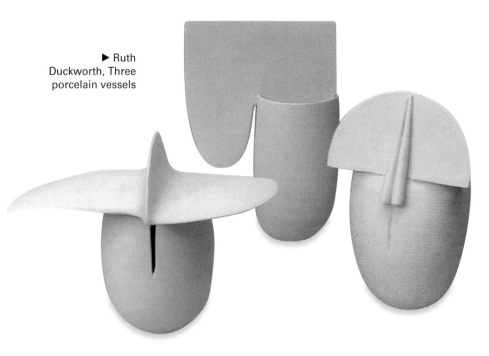

► Ruth Duckworth, Three porcelain vessels

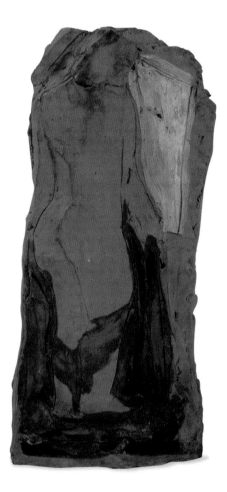

▲ Lucio Fontana, *Figura a la finestra*, polychrome slips, 1931. 15³/₄ x 7 x 8 inches (40 x 18 x 20 cm)

◄ Pompeo Pianezzola, Mural. 23¹/₂ x 13³/₄ x ³/₄ inches (60 x 35 x 1.8 cm). Stoneware with porcelain slip

The Second Half of the 20th Century

Around 1970, another medium (one based on the aesthetics of Minimalism, in which structure was of great importance and which promoted purity of shape to the utmost degree) was discovered: Land Art. This involved a new language that used nature as an arena for expression, and with which the concept of sculpture was broadened into a medium eligible for all kinds of liberties. In other words, sculpture expanded its uses and changed the direction of art to open up new opportunities in the areas of installation and action art. The latter was comprised of happenings and performances, processes that integrated the work of art into another dimension: time. Art was viewed as a part of life itself and turned life into a spectacle.

Installation artists include Anthony Gormley, T. Gragg, and Ryoji Koie, who create large assemblages of ceramic elements. In the field of action art, while they didn't use ceramics to a great extent, some of the Land Art practitioners (A. Mendieta, R. Long, A. Goldsworthy, and P. Noguera) actually used clay as a means of expression.

▲ Ángel Garraza, *Sites and Places*, 2000. Abandoibarra Park (Bilbao, Spain)

▼ Andy Goldsworthy, *Clay Wall*, 2004. 97$^{1}/_{2}$ x 446$^{1}/_{2}$ inches (248 x 1134 cm). The shrinkage in the clay caused the cracking.

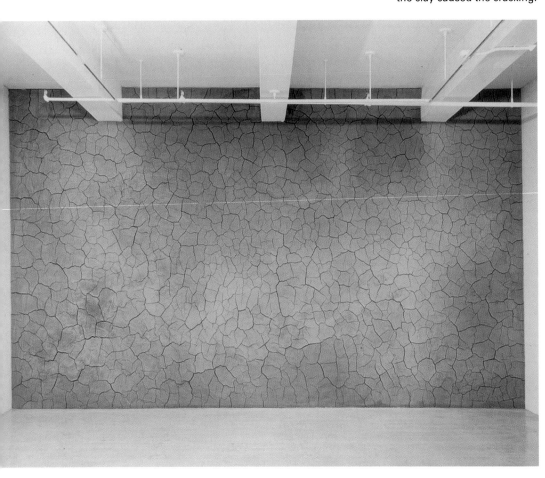

▼ Pere Noguera, *Mud*, 1980. Installation

When sculpture breaks through institutional barriers and becomes a part of the outdoors, the idea of the public space becomes a support for artistic endeavors, thereby creating what we now recognize as public sculpture. This is the context in which we can appreciate the works of such ceramists as B. Pepper, Ángel Garraza, Madola, and D. Dolz.

Once the avant-garde artists broke down the strict barriers of the academic institutions and their artificial separation of greater and lesser art, it became clear that no material is intrinsically art, yet it can be turned into an art object through the artist's intervention and the observer's interpretation.

Today, there are no materials unworthy of art, and we have gotten past the idea that sculpture has to be made of bronze and placed on a pedestal, just as R. Kraws predicted when he demonstrated the expanding concept of sculpture in the interdisciplinary, postmodern age.

▲ Madola, *Canal*, 1996. 33 x 21 x 19 inches (84 x 54 x 48 cm). Sculptural clay

▼ Anthony Gormley, *Field*, 1991. Spectacular terra-cotta installation

People often wonder how it was possible for humans at the beginning of civilization to make—with no experience, training, or technology—exceptional ceramic objects like those displayed in the best museums around the world.

The answer is that practice in handling the raw materials was surely what gave them the technical ability necessary to manage fire, water, and clays.

In this chapter, I will explain as simply as possible the most important characteristics of raw materials: minerals, plasticity, shrinkage, drying, porosity, and melting point. This will make it possible to understand the difference between clay in its raw state and a manufactured clay body, such as earthenware, stoneware, or porcelain. We also mustn't neglect the magic produced by the chemical reactions among the clay, glaze, and fire inside the kiln.

Raw
materials

Clays

The Origin of Clays

The term *clay* is applied to natural earth deposits that possess and display the singular property of plasticity. Clay is the product of the aging and decomposition of granite, feldspars, and pegmatites, which have been subjected to the actions of water, wind, glaciers, and plate tectonic movements over millions of years, plus the chemical action of the water, carbon dioxide, humic acids, and less commonly, sulfur and fluoride gases, aided by elevated temperatures.

Classifying Clays

Clays are classified in two categories: primary or residual, and secondary or sedimentary.

The primary clays are those that have remained in their original location after the original bedrock has been subjected to erosion from various forces.

Secondary clays have been transported far from their bedrock by water, atmospheric agents, or other means, and have been deposited in other places. The small particles of clay become grouped by size during the process, and they may mix with the products of other decomposed rocks. The heaviest particles are deposited as the transporting agent loses strength, while the lightest particles continue to travel and settle out, particularly in areas of calm or stagnant water. These clays are more plastic and very fine, although they may contain large quantities of organic matter and other minerals.

▲ Clay deposits are generally found in places with small hills; they are made up of layers about 7 feet (2 m) thick that may or may not be superimposed one on top of another. What's more, every time a new layer is discovered, the clay it contains may be of a different composition.

▶ Once the clays are extracted from the deposits, they are exposed to the elements for several years, piled up, and grouped according to their quality. A clay that has just been mined can't be worked right away; it must undergo an aging process outdoors.

▲ The chunks of clay stockpiled in the elements and subjected to the vagaries of weather freeze in the winter, and that helps break them down. Thus, as time passes, their plasticity improves.

Most clays come in a solid state from a quarry or mine, and are stored outdoors. Some plastic or soft clays can be extracted with shovels and excavators. Hard sculptural clays are extracted by first drilling holes and then using explosives to loosen the clay. Some primary kaolins that remain mixed in with the bedrock are removed with a strong blast of water.

Preparation

One of the processes that gives clay its plasticity is aging. The raw clay is stored outdoors for weeks, months, and even years, in all kinds of weather. In the winter, the water retained in the pores of the clay freezes and expands, and this breaks up the lumps.

The next step is grinding. The clay is fed through mills, where it is crushed, then mixed with water and set aside. Later, it is passed through vibrating sifters and moved through tubes to the hydraulic filter press to remove excess moisture. If the clay is to be kept moist, it is cut mechanically and sent by conveyor belts to the vacuum wedger, where it is wrapped in plastic.

▶ Most clays are extracted in large quantities with pneumatic shovels and trucks.

◀ A filter press removes excess water from the clay, then compresses the clay, leaving the correct amount of moisture.

▼ A vacuum wedger removes air bubbles and wraps the clay in plastic.

▲ When the clays come out of the filter press, they are placed in a wedger, which removes air bubbles.

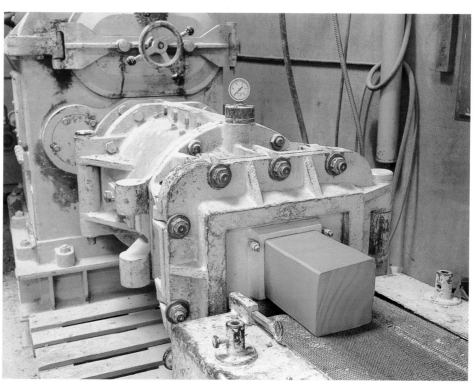

Classification of Clay Bodies

It's difficult to properly classify clays since by nature their composition and properties vary tremendously.

The term *clay* has a very broad meaning. In essence, clay is a natural, untreated product formed from a mixture of minerals such as kaolinite, chlorite, illite, and so forth, as well as minerals unrelated to clay, such as silicon, carbonates, feldspars, oxides, and more. Clays prepared industrially and ready for use by ceramists are known as *clay bodies*.

The raw materials used in preparing clay bodies are rarely pure substances. Therefore, a clay body is a specific mixture of raw, plastic, and refractory materials, which is ready for use by artists to create ceramic forms.

Ceramists need useful classifications applicable to their work, which has led to the proposal of criteria based on usage: terra cotta and sculptural clay bodies, as well as earthenware, stoneware, and porcelain.

It's important to know the chemical and mineral composition of the material being used because the composition determines its characteristics and the properties of the finished product. For instance, clay bodies become workable depending on the amount of plastic materials present. On the other hand, the inclusion of refractory materials keeps the work from shrinking too much and cracking during drying or firing. And the rigidity and shape retention of the piece during firing depend on the amount of flux and how it is mixed in.

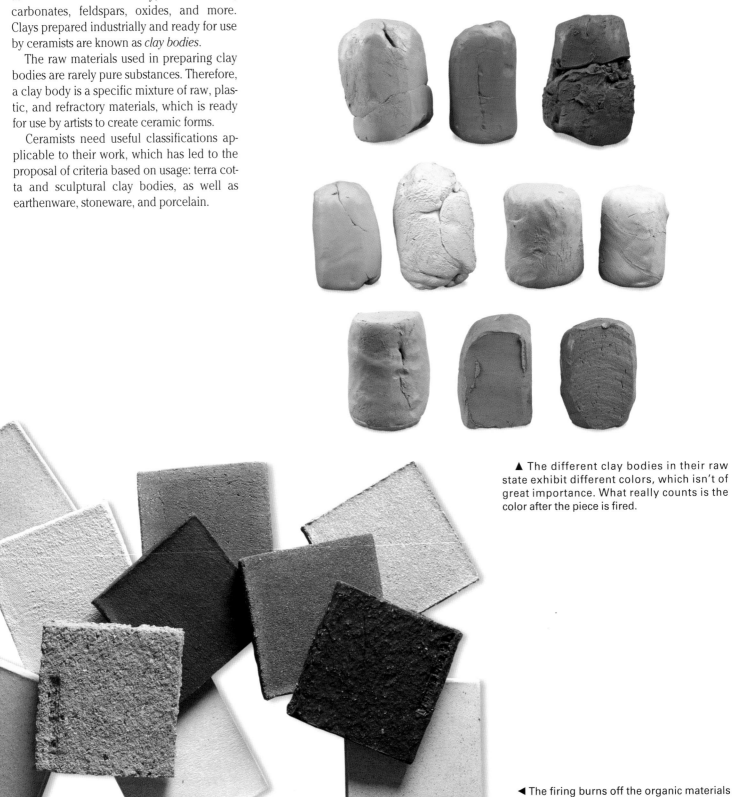

▲ The different clay bodies in their raw state exhibit different colors, which isn't of great importance. What really counts is the color after the piece is fired.

◄ The firing burns off the organic materials that produced the clay's color in its raw state.

Terra-Cotta Clay

The characteristics of these clays vary a great deal, depending on the location and the deposit from which they are drawn. They are of very fine quality and in general are prepared by aging in the fresh air or by grinding. In their natural state, they are generally dark reddish brown, due to the high content of iron oxide (Fe_2O_3)—about six to eight percent. Depending on the temperature and the atmosphere in the kiln, they take on a red or warm brown color after firing. These are highly fusible clays, so they typically aren't fired over 1922°F (1050°C). Because of their great plasticity, they are perfect for working on the wheel or for hand building small sculptures.

► ► Any type of work can be made from terra cotta. For murals, the size should not exceed 12 x 12 inches (30 x 30 cm), or $1/2$ to $3/4$ inch (1.5 to 2 cm) in thickness. Murals by Carlets, decorated with blue slip.

► Terra cotta. The high iron oxide content gives this clay its color; it is considered a low-temperature clay.

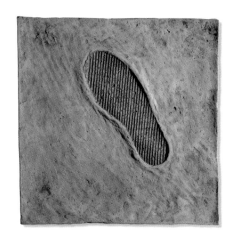

Scuptural clays

The sculptural clays are a difficult group to define. They are made up of various types of clays that contain a high proportion of alumina and silica.

Their properties vary widely according to their composition. They are resistant to high temperatures.

◄ Sculptural clay is ideal for large, complex creations, such as this figurative sculpture by Teresa Gironès.

► Sculptural clay makes it possible to create any kind of form, including solid ones, such as these works by Mercè Mir.

▲ Sculptural clays differ in color based on the type of clay from which they were prepared. They are recommended for any medium- or large-scale sculpture.

White Earthenware

White earthenware is difficult to find naturally, so ceramists often purchase commercially prepared clay bodies.

The composition of these clay bodies varies slightly, depending on the raw ingredients used to make them: clays, siliceous materials, or fluxes.

Plastic clays and kaolins make up the group of clays. For the siliceous materials, quartz is most commonly used because it is the most abundant. Among the fluxes, talc or frit is most common; the feldspathic fluxes include nepheline syenite and feldspar.

White clays have many possible uses. The most generic term used to designate low-temperature white clays is *white earthenware*. These are very plastic, porous bodies with a characteristic grayish color in their raw state, although after firing they are white.

They are often used to produce slip-cast forms, dishes, small sculptures, and wall tiles. Before applying glaze to a white earthenware vessel, a bisque firing should be done to about 1796°F (980°C).

▶ White earthenware is difficult to distinguish from white stoneware or porcelain after a bisque firing because they all fire to the same color.

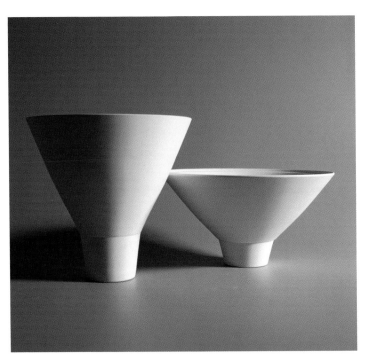

◀ Thrown bowls by Barbaformosa. Because low-fire white ware and high-fire white ware look identical after bisque firing, you must be careful to fire them at the correct temperatures. Low-fire ware will melt in a high-temperature firing and will ruin shelving.

▲ Joan Ramirez, *Gaudi*. White earthenware, underglaze, and crackle glaze.

▲ White bodies offer a broad range of possibilities for surface decoration without using a glaze, whether by firing with smoke or applying a patina, as seen in these forms by Barbaformosa.

Stoneware

Stoneware is a grayish white, opaque, vitrified clay body. It differs from terra cotta and white earthenware in color and firing range, and it is considered a high-temperature clay body. The firing range falls between 2192°F and 2372°F (1200°C and 1300°C).

Careful selection and correct proportions of clays, feldspars, and quartz, as well as the appropriate firing range, produce a vitrified stoneware with a low absorption rate. These bodies are sensitive to thermal shock, so they must be heated and cooled very slowly in order to avoid sudden thermal changes, especially in the case of large, thick pieces.

Their composition is approximately in the following proportions: 40 percent clays or kaolins; 30 percent feldspar and 30 percent quartz. In some instances, very fine grog is added (from 5 to 30 percent), which makes it possible to construct larger pieces both on and off the wheel. However, adding grog increases porosity and reduces vitrification. The final result depends in large part on the amount of grog added and on the final firing temperature. The higher the temperature, the greater the vitrification of the body, the harder it is, and the greater its resistance to scratching. Still, the firing must never exceed the final melting point of the clay body, since the pieces may warp or bloat.

▲ Stoneware in its natural state tends to be gray, but after the first bisque firing, turns buff.

◄ Functional stoneware form, with high-temperature glaze, fired to about 2300°F (1260°C), from the Rogenca studio

▲ This form by Antònia Roig demonstrates the decorative possibilities that stoneware offers when simple techniques, such as applying a colored glaze or sgraffito, are used.

◄ Utilitarian forms from the Rogenca studio. To work with stoneware, a little imagination is all that is needed.

CLAY BODIES				
CERÁMICS	Colored Clays	POROUS	Terra cota Sculptural clay Colored Clay	1742°F - 1992°F (950°C - 1050°C)
		VITRIFIED	Cone 6 white stoneware	2282°F - 2336°F (1250°C - 1280°C)
			Cone 6 dark stoneware	2282°F - 2336°F (1250°C - 1260°C)
	White Clays	POROUS	White earthenware	1796°F - 1922°F (980°C - 1050°C)
		VITRIFIED	Cone 10 white earthenware	2282°F - 2372°F 1250°C - 1300°C
			Porcelain	

▲ Porcelain bodies are white. One of their main characteristics is that they contain only small amounts of impurities from colorants such as iron oxide and titanium dioxide.

Porcelain

It is difficult to find pure kaolin that combines the necessary characteristics for good vitrification, translucency, and hardness in porcelain. For best results, choose an appropriate blend of clays or kaolins, feldspars, and silica.

Porcelain can be used to create utilitarian pieces as well as sculpture. Porcelain is white, vitreous, and translucent, although this last quality depends on the wall thickness. It is hard, acid-resistant, and has a less-than-one percent absorption rate.

Of concern when working with porcelain are the impurities of iron oxide, which completely alter the color. For that reason, artists working with porcelain should keep their studios clean, since any impurity from other clays can ruin the work.

◀▼ The translucent quality of porcelain can be seen in these lamps, which were made by Montse Seró using very thin slabs. A light source inside the lamps emphasizes their translucency.

◀ Maria Bofill, from the *Copas* series. Porcelain with copper red glaze, reduction fired.

Plasticity

This is a very complex quality that can be difficult to define. It is closely connected to the physical and chemical relationships among the particles in the clay, the water, and the among the particles themselves. As a result, it is influenced by the following five factors:

· Size and shape of clay particles
· Electrical attraction
· Carbonaceous matter and bacteria
· Water
· Aging

However, it's not enough to speak of the plasticity of clays from the chemical viewpoint. There is an easier way to define this characteristic: plasticity is the capacity of clay to absorb water, to be formed without rupturing or cracking, and to retain a shape.

In order for clays to exhibit this plasticity, there must be a fluid movement of particles over one another; and in order for them to retain their shape, there must be a certain amount of resistance to this flow. If the clay absorbs too much water, it will become a slip and lose its plasticity.

Such behavior doesn't exist in every state of the clay. For the clay to exhibit the proper plasticity, its water content must fall between certain values so that the clay is neither too dry or partially dry, nor so wet that it exhibits the characteristics of a slip. There is an easy way to test the plasticity of clays: take a piece of clay, roll it into a coil, and bend it. If it cracks, you have a short, or nonplastic, clay, and it will be difficult to work with; if it doesn't crack, it is plastic and can be worked into any shape.

Important materials in this group of plastic substances include some clays and kaolins.

◄ When coils crack, it means that the clay is very short and difficult to work with.

► When the clay is plastic, it is possible to work with it on the wheel without difficulty. Functional pieces from the Rogenca studio.

◄ When the coils exhibit no cracks, they are made from plastic clays.

Hardness

Raw refractory materials lack a plastic quality and thus have greatly reduced potential for being formed. It is difficult to make any object from them without causing cracking or warping. The plasticity of a clay body may be diminished by the addition of non-plastic raw materials—these reduce plasticity, shrinkage, and drying time. Among the most important ones are silica, feldspar, and grog.

▲ Made from a compact mass of clay, this is an interesting form by Pedro González.

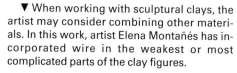

◄ This porcelain form by Yukiko Murata demonstrates the artist's great spontaneity, and once again confirms that this material allows the imagination to soar.

▼ When working with sculptural clays, the artist may consider combining other materials. In this work, artist Elena Montañés has incorporated wire in the weakest or most complicated parts of the clay figures.

Porosity

▼ This form by Ivet Bazaco was fired in reduction, using smoke techniques. The low-temperature firing means the piece remains porous.

Porosity is the ability of clay bodies to absorb water after firing. A pore is a tiny empty space surrounded by particles of clay. If a porous piece is submerged in water, it will absorb a great deal of it.

The most important items to keep in mind about porosity are closely linked to firing. The higher the firing temperature, the lower the porosity of the body. Porosity is common to all pieces fired at low temperatures, a fact that also affects glaze application. It's possible for porous objects to absorb more glaze than others, and as a result, alter the color or even cause the glaze to run. In that case, it's necessary to keep a standardized bisque temperature or to determine the optimum porosity of the clay body. (*Bisque firing* is the first firing—without glaze—to which the pieces are subjected.)

One of the most common methods to determine the porosity index of a clay body is to prepare a sample of the body, then bisque fire and weigh it. The sample is put in water and brought to a boil for two hours, then allowed to cool in the water for four hours. The surface is wiped dry and the piece is weighed again. The absorption percentage is as follows:

$$\frac{\text{Weight of wet clay body} - \text{Weight of bisqued clay body}}{\text{Weight of bisqued clay body}} \times 100$$

▶ After the bisque firing, all pieces are porous, regardless of their color and how they were made.

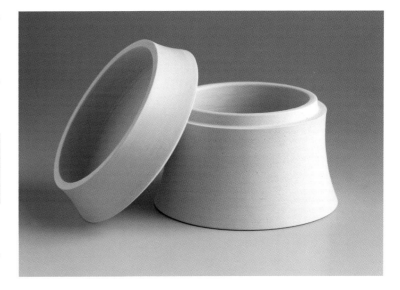

Shrinkage

The water that surrounds the clay particles and that makes the clay workable is water of plasticity; it makes up 20 to 35 percent of the weight of the wet clay. When the water evaporates, the particles of clay move closer together, and the entire piece shrinks. The smaller the particles, the greater the shrinkage, and thus the greater the risk that the piece will become distorted or cracked. The final size of the work will be slightly smaller because it loses all of this water.

Ceramic work loses all of its water during two processes: the drying, in which the clay loses its water of plasticity and becomes leather hard; and the firing, when the clay loses the remaining water, which is referred to as chemical water. During the firing, the clay shrinks permanently.

To calculate the shrinkage that clay bodies undergo from the time they are wet to the point of total shrinkage, proceed as follows: Make a slab from moist clay measuring $^1/_3$ x 1 $^1/_4$ x 4 $^3/_4$ inches (1 x 3 x 12 cm) and mark a scale 4 inches (0 to 10 cm) long. After firing, measure the scale and calculate the percentage of shrinkage. The shrinkage of clay bodies can be approximately summarized in the following way:

▶ This piece demonstrates what happens when there is a difference in shrinkage between a body and a glaze: cracks appear. However, in this work, artist Joan Serra took advantage of the series of cracks to make a very interesting piece.

◀ To determine the shrinkage of a piece of clay, make a sample slab and mark a line 4 inches (10 cm) long on it. After firing, measure the line to determine the difference. Today, it's not necessary to determine the shrinkage of clays with this method, since boxes of clay now indicate all of its characteristics. If they don't, contact the distributor.

Terra cotta . . . . .6%–8% firing to 1832°F–1868°F (1000°C–1020°C)
Earthenware . . . . .8%–10% firing to 1832°F–1868°F (1000°C–1020°C)
Stoneware .10%–15% firing to 2282°F–2372°F (1250°C–1280°C)
Porcelain . . . . .10%–15% firing to 2282°F–2372°F (1350°C–1400°C)

The tools that a ceramist needs for working are very simple and can easily be purchased or made. In this chapter, the necessary tools and their uses will be discussed. It can be said that in learning to work with clay, all that is needed is a strong interest. But it is crucial to be relaxed when working so you can develop your creativity. It's a good idea, therefore, to have a small space where you can practice in peace. You'll need a table, a stool, and all the tools ready and within easy reach. If you have to get up every time you need a tool, you will waste time and lose your concentration. In this chapter, tools are organized according to specialties. Also discussed are firing methods, types of kilns, and at what points in the firing it is possible to speed up or slow down the process. To do so, the firing curves must be read very carefully.

Tools
and Their Uses

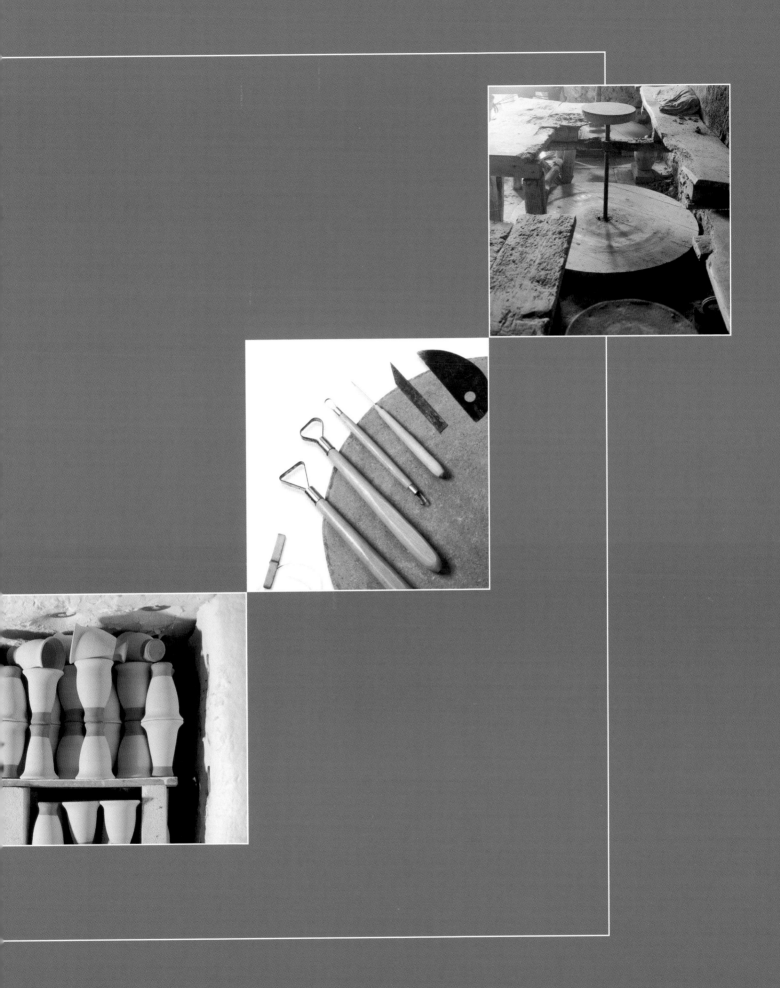

Tools and Equipment

While the hands are very important in clay work, tools are very useful as well. It is important to have a number of tools on hand that you have bought or made yourself. The wire loop tools are probably the most difficult to replicate, but it's easy to come up with wooden shaping

Starting Out

Banding Wheel

The banding wheel is very useful when coil building, applying glaze or slip with a brush, and so forth. It's an essential tool and one of the first that should be bought.

Canvas Cloth

Slabs should be worked on a table or similar surface. To keep the clay from sticking, cover the worktable with a piece of cloth and work with the clay on that. Using a stiff cloth will avoid creating wrinkles or folds in the clay.

Rollers

A simple kitchen rolling pin can be used to roll out small slabs. Made of turned hardwood, special rollers for clay tend to be much larger and sturdier. When rolled over the clay, they absorb water, preventing the clay from sticking to the wood.

Wood Strips

Wood strips are used in pairs, along with the roller and the canvas, to form clay slabs of various thicknesses. They can also be used as straightedges and as supports for work made from slabs.

Cutting Wire

This may be made of very thin nylon or steel. Usually, a piece of wood is attached to each end for use as handles. The wire is stretched tight when cutting clay that has come from a package or that has recently been thrown.

Spray Bottle

It's common not to finish hand building a piece in a single day, and it may even take three or four days. When you return to work, you may discover that some areas of the work have dried out. To avoid this, use a spray bottle to mist the driest parts of the piece and cover the piece with plastic. The moisture is then retained until the following day.

Plastic Bags

The main problem with clay is that it begins to dry as soon as it comes into contact with air, and then becomes difficult to work with. To prevent this from happening, cover the clay with a plastic trash bag at the end of the workday. If you will not be working with the piece for a while, moisten it by spraying the surface with water before covering it up with the bag, making it as airtight as possible.

Slab Roller

A slab roller is used to make slabs of clay of a consistent size and thickness. In addition, it's much quicker than using a wooden roller and wood strips.

▼ A banding wheel is helpful when brushing glaze or slip on the surface of a form.

▲ These tools are essential when making clay slabs: wood strips (A), roller (B), cutting wire (C), plastic trash bags (D), and a spray bottle (E).

Shaping and Smoothing

Modeling Tools

Modeling tools are essential. They can be used to shape as well as to smooth a hard-to-reach surface of the pot. Generally, they are made of wood, but there are also modeling tools made of metal, plastic, and other materials.

It's a good idea to have modeling tools of various shapes so you can use the one best suited to the surface you're working with, and reach all areas of the piece.

Trimming Tools

These are used to remove excess clay from the surface. They are used in a number of techniques, so they are often needed. Straight trimming tools are commonly used for smoothing pieces and rounded ones for hollowing them out.

Ribs

These tools are necessary for all kinds of techniques. They can be used to smooth and burnish the surface of a piece, to remove excess clay from a vessel, and even to clean the worktable. They may come in different shapes and thicknesses, and are made of various materials, such as metal, wood, plastic, or rubber.

Saw Blade

The saw blade can be used for cutting, smoothing, scratching, texturing, and more. It consists of a piece of hacksaw blade adapted to the potter's requirements.

Brushes

Brushes can be used often. Knowing which type of brush to use at any time can save money, for artists often use higher-quality, higher-priced brushes than are necessary.

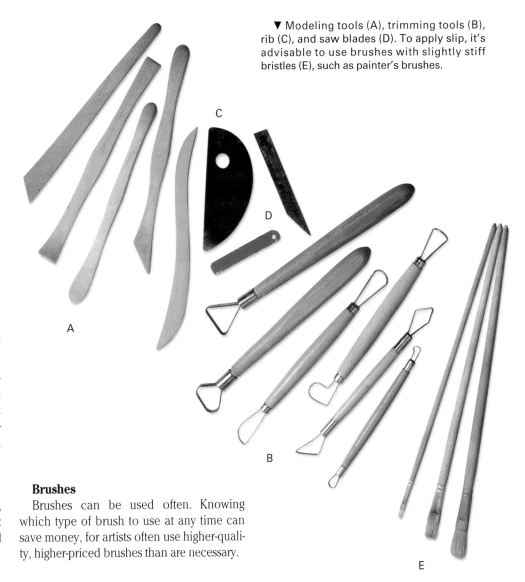

▼ Modeling tools (A), trimming tools (B), rib (C), and saw blades (D). To apply slip, it's advisable to use brushes with slightly stiff bristles (E), such as painter's brushes.

▼ A slab roller can make slabs of consistent sizes and thicknesses.

Mold-Making Tools

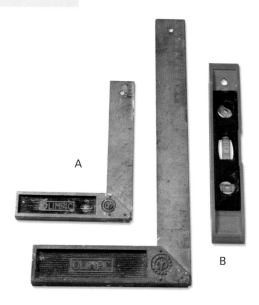

▲ Metal squares (A) and level (B)

The tools used for making molds are very basic. While there are tools made specifically for this purpose, many tools from other areas of clay work can be easily adapted to mold making.

Necessary Tools

Squares and Level

The square can be made of any material. It's used for many purposes, such as making sure the base of a piece is perpendicular to the table. The level can be used to make sure that lines are horizontal and that any two points are at the same height.

Plastic or Rubber Buckets

Containers used in working with plaster should be made from a flexible material, since that makes the containers easier to clean by striking them until the dried plaster flakes off.

Mold Soap

Mold soap and a release agent are needed to aid in the removal of the work from the mold.

Scale

A scale is another tool that every potter should have on hand when working with plaster. It is used for weighing water or plaster. A highly accurate scale is not needed for making molds; a kitchen scale, preferably digital, works well.

Metal Modeling Tools

Iron or stainless-steel modeling tools are best for mold making because it's often necessary to touch up a mold after the plaster has dried completely, and the required tools need to be strong and sharp.

Trimming Tools

Several round trimming tools are needed for making molds. They carve out the registration marks that hold the mold parts together.

◀ Trimming tools

▲ Rubber and plastic buckets used for mixing plaster and making molds

◀ Metal shaping tools and ribs

Mold-Finishing Tools

Some very simple tools are used for finishing molds: a backsaw, a whisk broom, and a wire brush. The saw is used for removing weight and perfecting the outside finish. The wire brush is used to clean the whisk broom, which becomes clogged very quickly when it's used to finish the plaster.

Plywood or Plastic Laminate

To cover a piece with liquid plaster, a structure is made with plywood boards or pieces of plastic laminate measuring about 8 x 14 inches (20 x 35 cm). The work is placed in the center of this structure and the plaster is poured. The plywood boards or plastic laminates are held together with clamps or straps. Plastic laminates are very easy materials to clean and are resistant to moisture.

Clamps

Also referred to as C-clamps or bar clamps, these are very useful for holding together the plywood structure while the plaster is setting. Mold straps can also be used instead of clamps.

Knives, Chisels, and Mallet

Putty knives are very useful tools, and every ceramist should have several made of metal or rubber. They are used to adjust the plaster when making a lost wax mold or when smoothing and finishing molds. A good utility knife for beveling the edges of the molds is also a must. Chisels—just like the ones used in woodworking—are used for trimming edges and indexing molds. In mold making, they are used to break apart the finished mold by carefully driving the chisel with a mallet.

Brushes

The brushes used for mold making should have synthetic bristles. Several sizes of the cheapest painter's brushes on the market are adequate. They are used to apply the mold soap to the original and to the mold, and for cleaning the work surfaces.

Plastic Containers

Before beginning work, it's a good idea to prepare a few plastic or glass containers to make the soap mixtures, to hold water for cleaning the mold, and to use as receptacles for excess clay that's become contaminated with plaster.

▲ Backsaw (A), perforated rasps (B), and wire brush (C)

▲ Metal putty knives (A) and bench knife (B)

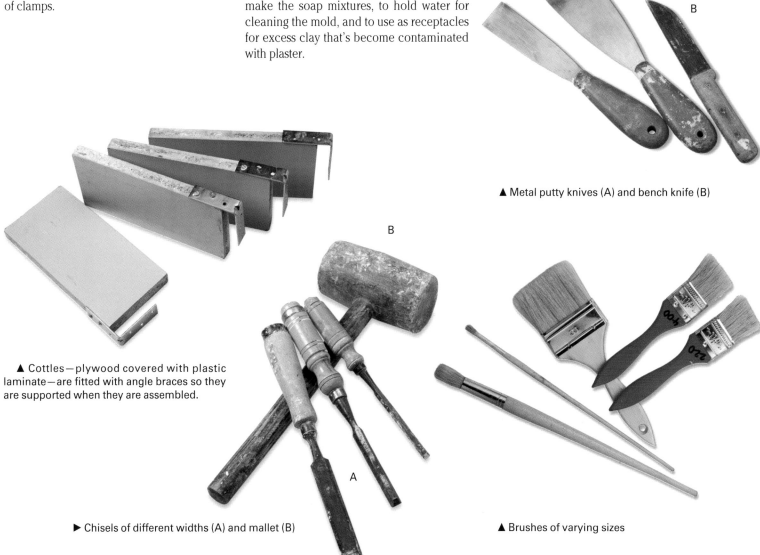

▲ Cottles—plywood covered with plastic laminate—are fitted with angle braces so they are supported when they are assembled.

▶ Chisels of different widths (A) and mallet (B)

▲ Brushes of varying sizes

35

Tools and Equipment for Throwing on the Wheel

The Potter's Wheel

The potter's wheel is the main tool for most ceramists, since it makes it possible to produce pieces quickly and conveniently, and enables them to build up inventory quickly.

There are several types of wheels, but they all consist of a round wheel head attached to a vertical axis on which the wheel head turns. The throwing is done in the center of the wheel head. The wheel may be powered by foot or by an electric motor.

The kick wheel has been used by potters for centuries. However, in many places it has been almost entirely replaced by the electric wheel. The advantages of electric wheels include their smaller size, adjustable speed, and the possibility of quicker production, which provides a competitive edge. Many ceramists have also fitted an electric motor to their kick wheels, but the performance of these modified kick wheels can't compare to that of small electric wheels.

Kick wheels have been replaced by electric ones that are smaller in size and easy to transport. This type of wheel can be placed in any corner of the studio, and has been a great convenience for ceramists who don't have a lot of space in their studios.

Pug Mill

A pug mill is a machine that wedges clay. It helps the ceramist avoid the fatigue of wedging by hand. Pug mills have an electric motor, with a loading hopper and a lever for squeezing the clay, which help prevent any injuries. Nevertheless, it's a good idea to become familiar with wedging by hand because many small studios do not have pug mills. During the learning stage, it's advisable to wedge the clay by hand. Once you are producing a large body of work, you may feel the need for a pug mill.

◀ Electric wheel

▼ Kick wheel

▼ A pug mill is used to wedge and compact the clay.

Throwing Bats

As you progress in ceramics, a single wheel head is not enough, since some pieces can't be removed from the wheel until they are leather hard, and that slows down the pace of work. To solve this problem, potters can construct or buy several round bats made of wood, plaster, or thick plastic, and place them on the wheel head for throwing. Thus, the thrown pot can remain on the bat when it is removed from the wheel.

Calipers

These are very useful when working on the wheel. Calipers are commonly used to measure the mouths and lids of teapots, as well as the height of pieces that must be the same. There are many types of calipers, and they are all equally useful.

Trimming Tools

Trimming tools have a straight or rounded cutting edge, and all have a beveled cutting edge that makes it easier to remove excess clay from the piece. When you want a straight angle on the foot of the piece, you use the straight cutting edge; when you want a rounded foot, you use the rounded cutting edge.

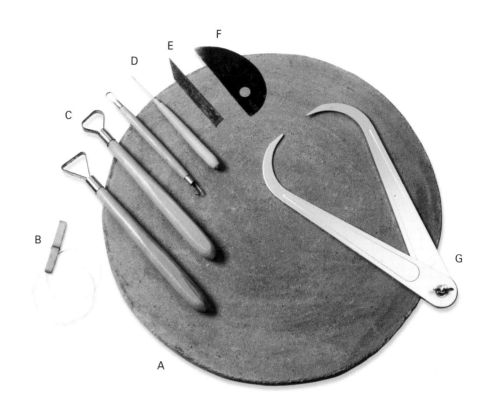

▲ A wooden bat (A), cutting wire (B), trimming tools (C), needle tool (D), hacksaw blade (E), rib (F), and calipers (G)

▼ This kick wheel has had an electric motor fitted to it.

Needle Tools

A metal needle tool is used to incise decoration on the surface of a piece or to sign the work once it's finished. Needle tools have many applications, and they are essential in the studio.

Wedging Board

Because wedging is so important, the studio must have a plaster slab for wedging clays while they are still somewhat moist. A plaster wedging board can easily be made: Spread out a piece of plastic on the floor and place four boards around it. The boards are connected with clamps and the corners are sealed with wads of clay. Pour liquid plaster inside the boards to form a layer 1 to 2 inches (3 to 5 cm) thick, and place burlap over this entire layer. Then pour the rest of the plaster to a thickness of 3 to 4 inches (8 to 10 cm). After drying for 24 hours, the wedging board is ready to absorb the water from the clay.

Glazing and Decorating Tools

Necessary Tools

Precision Scale

In ceramics, it is very important to prepare glazes precisely, and special care is required in weighing the ingredients. Therefore, a precision scale is necessary. Although many models are available, it is preferable to use manual scales for weighing oxides and colorants, which require precision. In weighing quantities over 3 1/2 ounces (100 g), you can use digital scales, which have a small margin of error (.02 ounce to .04 ounce/0.5 g to 1.0 g).

Sieves

Sieves are essential for straining glaze ingredients—they remove any foreign material and lumps. There are meshes of different sizes, which are designated by numbers on the sieves; the higher the number, the finer the mesh. It is very important always to sieve the glazes.

Blender

When making glazes, ceramists use a hand blender. This tool mixes up glazes very quickly and makes them homogenous. Before glazing any work, the glaze ingredients should be mixed or ground, then sieved.

Bulb Syringe

These rubber syringes are commonly used for slip trailing. They also have many other uses in the workshop, such as decorating with glaze, adding water to mixtures, and so forth. In order to prevent unwanted crossover between products and the possibility of making mistakes, bulbs should be cleaned thoroughly after each use. It's a good idea to have two or three different sizes, if possible.

Mortar and Pestle

Although a blender meets most mixing needs, a mortar and pestle are used to grind oxides or colorants into finer mesh sizes. The mortar must be made of a hard material, such as porcelain or glass.

▼ A variety of tools used in glazing: sieves of different mesh sizes (A), precision scales (B), hand blender (C), dipping tongs (D), spoons (E), brushes (F), plastic cups (G), and a rubber bulb syringe (H)

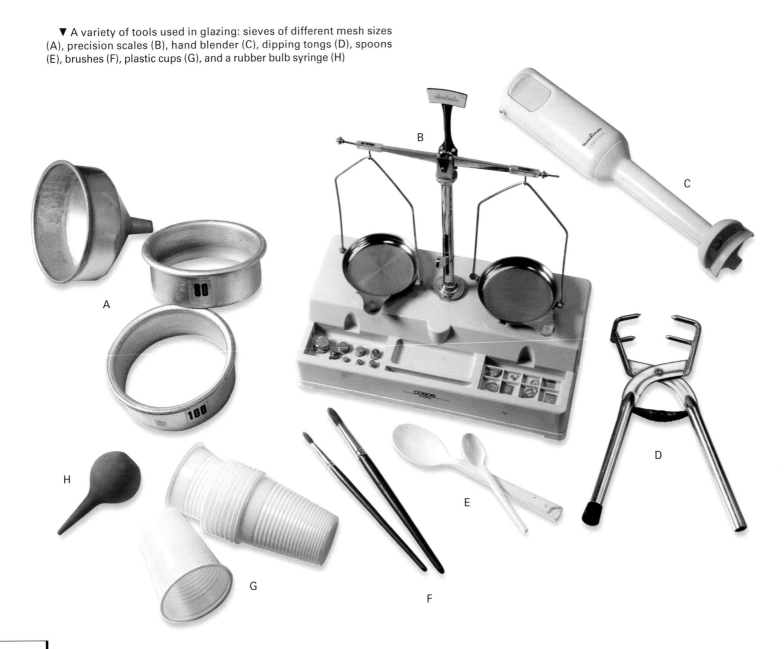

Spoons and Cups

The studio must have some spoons, cups, and labels. The spoons can be used to transfer materials for weighing. The plastic cups hold the product, and the labels are used to number and identify samples.

Dipping Tongs

Dipping tongs are used to hold a piece when it's dipped into a container of glaze. This speeds up the glazing process and prevents leaving fingerprints on the surface.

Brushes

Very fine, flat bristle brushes are used for glazing with broad strokes. Often, the base of the piece is left unglazed for a decorative effect. Round, broad brushes with synthetic bristles can be used to mix glazes in liquid form. Round boar's bristle brushes can be used for glazing that requires greater detail, as well as for drip applications. Sash brushes and flat brushes are ideal for glazing broad areas.

Brushes need to be kept in perfect condition. Even if the bristles are synthetic, it is important to clean and preserve them. They are stored either flat or vertical with the bristles pointing upward.

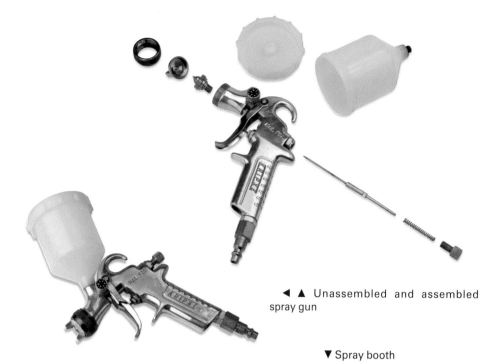

◄ ▲ Unassembled and assembled spray gun

▼ Spray booth

▲ Mask for protection against dust and dry ingredients

Spray Gun and Compressor

For spraying glaze on a pot, it's essential to have a spray gun, preferably with a top-mounted reservoir, as well as a compressor that's not too large and that's equipped with an air tank. The spray gun should be used in a spray booth with an exhaust fan. When spraying glaze, the potter should always wear a dust mask or respirator. The spray gun must be cleaned after every use by taking it apart completely and cleaning all pieces with a rag moistened with oil. The spray gun is stored unassembled.

Spray Booth

Spray booths are generally made of metal or plastic, with an exhaust fan installed at the top. This works like a kitchen fan, removing the particles released by the spray gun.

These booths are essential when spraying glaze because they remove the toxic particles from the studio. If you don't have a booth, you can glaze by dipping in a glaze bath or by using a brush.

▲ Compressor

Kilns and Firing Methods

Kilns

Inside the kiln, a series of physical and chemical transformations takes place during the firing process.

There are different types of kilns, and the choice of which to use depends on the desired results. There are, however, two general types based on the fuel used: gas and electric. Both are installed in accordance with local regulations.

Electric Kiln

Electric kilns have several advantages, including ease of use and energy efficiency. In addition, today they are all equipped with an automatic digital controller that controls the firing process. The data for the desired firing can be programmed into the controller, and the kiln does all the work itself. Before buying an electric kiln, you must check the voltage in your studio; some small kilns generally work with household current, though.

Gas Kiln

It's not difficult to work with gas, but it requires a more elaborate setup. The kiln is lined with ceramic fiber. The entire firing requires constant vigilance and monitoring of the gas and air pressure in the burners. These kilns can reach maximum temperature in eight to twelve hours. Depending on their size, they are equipped with two, four, or six burners that generally are installed in the side walls or the floor of the kiln. These kilns can be natural draft or forced air, and can be downdraft, updraft, or crossdraft. The greatest advantage of a gas kiln is the ability to fire in an oxidation or reduction atmosphere.

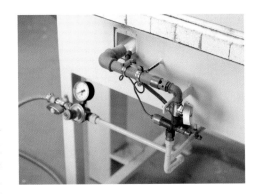

▲ Detail of a gas kiln burner

▲ Gas kilns equipped with four and six burners, respectively

▶ This front-loading kiln has heating coils in the walls and the door. It can reach a temperature of 2444°F (1340°C).

▼ This top-loading electric kiln can reach a temperature of 2300°F (1260°C).

▶ This kiln was made especially for raku, but it can be used for normal firing at high or low temperatures.

When you buy a kiln, you need to purchase the necessary furniture and accessories for use in firing. You must also determine if you will be working at high or low temperatures.

Furniture and Accessories

Stilts

Triangular in shape, stilts are used to raise the pieces off the kiln shelves, which prevents sticking. They may be made of porcelain, although these break easily when struck, or of kanthal, the same metal alloy used for the heating elements in the kiln. The metal stilts last indefinitely, but they can be used only at low temperatures.

Kiln Shelves

Kiln shelves are made from refractory material; the work is placed on them for firing inside the kiln. If the firing is low temperature, the shelves can be of cordierite; they are thinner than standard shelves and cool quickly. For a high-temperature firing, the shelves are made with higher proportions of alumina and silicon carbide, and they take much longer to cool. To protect the shelves from glaze drippings, they are covered with the following kiln wash: 40 percent alumina, 40 percent kaolin, and 20 percent silica.

Kiln Posts

These supports separate the shelves inside the kiln; they can be used in low and high temperatures. Some are made of silicon carbide; others are columns made of refractory material. They can also be made from high-density refractory bricks cut to the desired dimensions.

Tile Setters

Tile setters made of refractory material make it possible to fire a large number of tiles in a small space. These are available from ceramics suppliers. They are very useful for firing murals or glazed floor and wall tiles.

Plate Setters

Tripods made of refractory clays are used as holders for firing plates one on top of another, thereby making good use of the space inside the kiln.

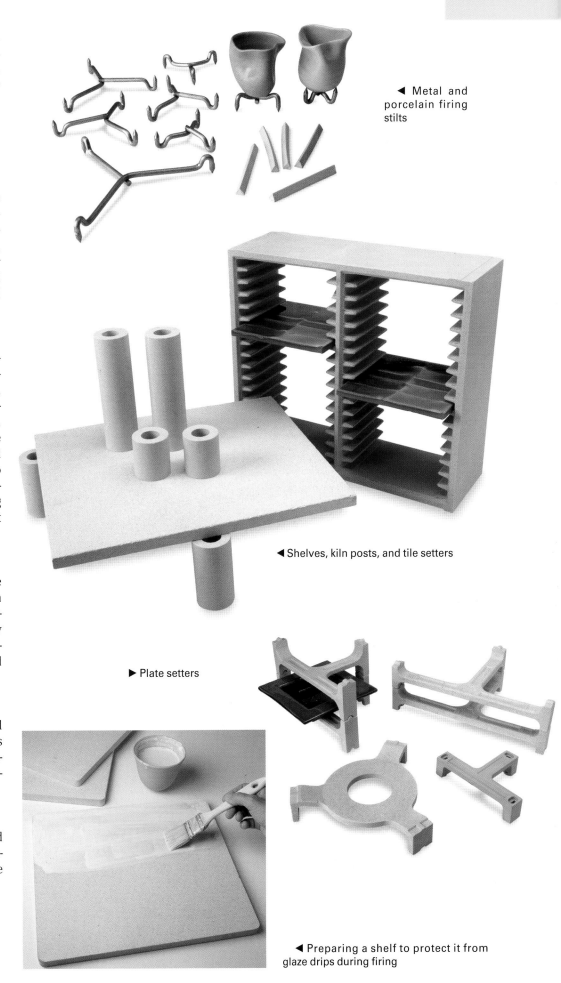

◄ Metal and porcelain firing stilts

◄ Shelves, kiln posts, and tile setters

► Plate setters

◄ Preparing a shelf to protect it from glaze drips during firing

SEGER PYROMETRIC CONE FORMULAS

Melt Point °F/°C	Cone	Chemical Composition					
1112/600	022						
1202/650	021	0.5 Na$_2$O	0.25 CaO	0.25 MgO	0.02 Al$_2$O$_3$	1.0 B$_2$O$_3$	1.04 SiO$_2$
1238/670	020	0.5 Na$_2$O	0.25 CaO	0.25 MgO	0.04 Al$_2$O$_3$	1.0 B$_2$O$_3$	1.08 SiO$_2$
1274/690	019	0.5 Na$_2$O	0.25 CaO	0.25 MgO	0.08 Al$_2$O$_3$	1.0 B$_2$O$_3$	1.16 SiO$_2$
1310/710	018	0.5 Na$_2$O	0.25 CaO	0.25 MgO	0.13 Al$_2$O$_3$	1.0 B$_2$O$_3$	1.26 SiO$_2$
1346/730	017	0.5 Na$_2$O	0.25 CaO	0.25 MgO	0.20 Al$_2$O$_3$	1.0 B$_2$O$_3$	1.40 SiO$_2$
1382/750	016	0.5 Na$_2$O	0.25 CaO	0.25 MgO	0.31 Al$_2$O$_3$	1.0 B$_2$O$_3$	1.61 SiO$_2$
1454/790	015a	0.432 Na$_2$O	0.432 CaO	0.136 MgO	0.34 Al$_2$O$_3$	0.86 B$_2$O$_3$	2.06 SiO$_2$
1499/815	014a	0.385 Na$_2$O	0.385 CaO	0.230 MgO	0.34 Al$_2$O$_3$	0.77 B$_2$O$_3$	1.92 SiO$_2$
1535/835	013a	0.343 Na$_2$O	0.343 CaO	0.314 MgO	0.34 Al$_2$O$_3$	0.69 B$_2$O$_3$	1.78 SiO$_2$
1571/855	012a	0.345 Na$_2$O	0.341 CaO	0.314 MgO	0.355 Al$_2$O$_3$	0.68 B$_2$O$_3$	2.04 SiO$_2$
1616/880	011a	0.349 Na$_2$O	0.340 CaO	0.311 MgO	0.400 Al$_2$O$_3$	0.68 B$_2$O$_3$	2.38 SiO$_2$
1652/900	010a	-	-	-	-	-	-
1688/920	09a	0.5 Na$_2$O	0.5 PbO	-	0.8 Al$_2$O$_3$	0.1 B$_2$O$_3$	3.6 SiO$_2$
1724/940	08a	0.3 K$_2$O	0.7 CaO	0.2 Fe$_2$O$_3$	0.3 Al$_2$O$_3$	0.5 B$_2$O$_3$	3.5 SiO$_2$
1760/960	07a	0.5 K$_2$O	0.7 CaO	0.2 Fe$_2$O$_3$	0.3 Al$_2$O$_3$	0.45 B$_2$O$_3$	3.55 SiO$_2$
1796/980	06a	0.3 K$_2$O	0.7 CaO	0.2 Fe$_2$O$_3$	0.3 Al$_2$O$_3$	0.40 B$_2$O$_3$	3.60 SiO$_2$
1832/1000	05a	0.3 K$_2$O	0.7 CaO	0.2 Fe$_2$O$_3$	0.3 Al$_2$O$_3$	0.35 B$_2$O$_3$	3.65 SiO$_2$
1868/1020	04a	0.3 K$_2$O	0.7 CaO	0.2 Fe$_2$O$_3$	0.3 Al$_2$O$_3$	0.30 B$_2$O$_3$	3.70 SiO$_2$
1904/1040	03a	0.3 K$_2$O	0.7 CaO	0.2 Fe$_2$O$_3$	0.3 Al$_2$O$_3$	0.25 B$_2$O$_3$	3.75 SiO$_2$
1940/1060	02a	0.3 K$_2$O	0.7 CaO	0.2 Fe$_2$O$_3$	0.3 Al$_2$O$_3$	0.20 B$_2$O$_3$	3.80 SiO$_2$
1976/1080	01a	0.3 K$_2$O	0.7 CaO	0.2 Fe$_2$O$_3$	0.3 Al$_2$O$_3$	0.10 B$_2$O$_3$	3.85 SiO$_2$
2012/1100	1a	0.3 K$_2$O	0.7 CaO	0.2 Fe$_2$O$_3$	0.3 Al$_2$O$_3$	0.05 B$_2$O$_3$	3.90 SiO$_2$
2048/1120	2a	0.3 K$_2$O	0.7 CaO	0.2 Fe$_2$O$_3$	0.3 Al$_2$O$_3$	-	3.95 SiO$_2$
2084/1140	3a	0.3 K$_2$O	0.7 CaO	0.2 Fe$_2$O$_3$	0.3 Al$_2$O$_3$	-	4.0 SiO$_2$
2120/1160	4a	0.3 K$_2$O	0.7 CaO	0.1 Fe$_2$O$_3$	0.4 Al$_2$O$_3$	-	4.0 SiO$_2$
2156/1180	5a	0.3 K$_2$O	0.7 CaO	0.05 Fe$_2$O$_3$	0.45 Al$_2$O$_3$	-	4.0 SiO$_2$
2192/1200	6a	0.3 K$_2$O	0.7 CaO	-	0.50 Al$_2$O$_3$	-	4.0 SiO$_2$
2246/1230	7	0.3 K$_2$O	0.7 CaO	-	0.50 Al$_2$O$_3$	-	5.0 SiO$_2$
2282/1250	8	0.3 K$_2$O	0.7 CaO	-	0.60 Al$_2$O$_3$	-	6.0 SiO$_2$
2336/1280	9	0.3 K$_2$O	0.7 CaO	-	0.70 Al$_2$O$_3$	-	7.0 SiO$_2$
2372/1300	10	0.3 K$_2$O	0.7 CaO	-	0.80 Al$_2$O$_3$	-	8.0 SiO$_2$
2408/1320	11	0.3 K$_2$O	0.7 CaO	-	0.90 Al$_2$O$_3$	-	9.0 SiO$_2$
2462/1350	12	0.3 K$_2$O	0.7 CaO	-	1.0 Al$_2$O$_3$	-	10.0 SiO$_2$
2516/1380	13	0.3 K$_2$O	0.7 CaO	-	1.2 Al$_2$O$_3$	-	12.0 SiO$_2$
2570/1410	14	0.3 K$_2$O	0.7 CaO	-	1.4 Al$_2$O$_3$	-	14.0 SiO$_2$
2615/1435	15	0.3 K$_2$O	0.7 CaO	-	1.6 Al$_2$O$_3$	-	16.0 SiO$_2$
2660/1460	16	0.3 K$_2$O	0.7 CaO	-	1.8 Al$_2$O$_3$	-	18.0 SiO$_2$
2696/1480	17	0.3 K$_2$O	0.7 CaO	-	2.1 Al$_2$O$_3$	-	21.0 SiO$_2$
2732/1500	18	0.3 K$_2$O	0.7 CaO	-	3.1 Al$_2$O$_3$	-	31.0 SiO$_2$
2768/1520	19	0.3 K$_2$O	0.7 CaO	-	3.5 Al$_2$O$_3$	-	35.0 SiO$_2$
2786/1530	20	0.3 K$_2$O	0.7 CaO	-	3.9 Al$_2$O$_3$	-	39.0 SiO$_2$
2876/1580	26	0.3 K$_2$O	0.7 CaO	-	7.2 Al$_2$O$_3$	-	72.0 SiO$_2$
2930/1610	27	0.3 K$_2$O	0.7 CaO	-	20.0 Al$_2$O$_3$	Kaolín	200.0 SiO$_2$
2966/1630	28	-	-	-	1.0 Al$_2$O$_3$	-	10.0 SiO$_2$
3002/1650	29	-	-	-	1.0 Al$_2$O$_3$	-	8.0 SiO$_2$
3038/1670	30	-	-	-	1.0 Al$_2$O$_3$	-	66.0 SiO$_2$
3074/1690	31	-	-	-	1.0 Al$_2$O$_3$	-	5.0 SiO$_2$
3110/1710	32	-	-	-	1.0 Al$_2$O$_3$	-	4.0 SiO$_2$
3146/1730	33	-	-	-	1.0 Al$_2$O$_3$	-	-

Digital Controller

Electric kilns are equipped with digital controllers that can store up to 100 different firing cycles. They can also be purchased and installed on existing kilns. These devices makes it possible to program the desired firing temperatures, thus freeing up the ceramist from continually watching over the kiln. Still, controllers are subject to variation, and it's possible that the temperature indicated won't correspond to the one inside the kiln. To determine the difference between the indicated and the actual temperatures, cones should be used during the initial firings because they are precise.

Cones

These are pyramid-shaped temperature indicators with a number on one side. Also known as pyrometric cones, they are made of a specially formulated ceramic material that melts at a specific temperature in relation to a specific temperature rise. They are placed inside the kiln at an 82–degree angle. That tilt allows the cones to bend as they reach the indicated temperature. They are lined up with the spy hole commonly located in the center of the kiln door. During firing, it is possible to see the moment when the cones bend, so the kiln can be turned off. Protective eyewear should be worn to protect the eyes from the light and the heat of the fire.

▼ The various phases cones go through from the time they are put into the kiln through the completion of firing: The first cone on the left, which is inclined at 82 degrees, indicates prefiring. As the temperature slowly rises, the cone bends slightly, as shown in the second row. When the firing is complete, the tip of the cone should touch the kiln shelf, as shown in the third row. And when the temperature is exceeded, the cone melts, as in the row at the far right.

◀ A good digital controller makes it possible to easily program a firing for day or night.

Firing Clay Bodies

The proper firing temperature for a clay body depends on many factors, especially its chemical composition, the peak temperature and the length of soak, the duration of the firing, and the cooling. It is important to understand the concept of firing clay work to the correct temperature.

Maturity

This refers to the optimum point reached by clays during the final firing. All clay bodies have a specific shrinkage and absorption rate determined for their firing range. If the clay is not fired high enough, it will have a high absorption rate or remain porous. If it is fired higher, it will become vitrified with a lower absorption rate. If fired too high, it will slump or bloat.

Melting Point

All clay bodies have a specific melting point at which they soften, and if the temperature is excessive, they progressively turn from a solid to a liquid state. In this process, the piece begins to gradually slump and may lose its shape altogether. When buying clay bodies, it's important to know their melting points, and thus the temperatures to stay below unless aiming for an artistic effect.

◀ In this sculpture by Joan Serra, the cracks formed by shrinkage are used as a decorative effect.

▶ Detail of the piece: Cracks that occurred during the firing process are clearly visible.

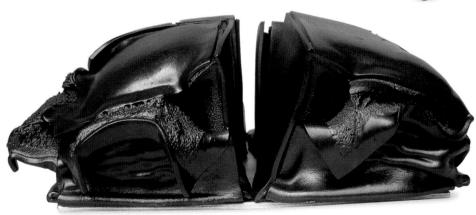

◀▲ Two views of a sculpture in which the meaning of melting point is clearly visible. The clay slumps and eventually turns into a liquid mass. In this example, artist Joan Serra has sought the precise melting point to create a sculpture from a firing defect.

Chemical Composition

This concept refers to the chemical compounds that alter the melting point of a clay body. The firing range of a clay body is not the same as the melting point, and the latter depends in large part on the fluxes in the clay body. Among the most significant ones are iron oxide, calcium compounds, and feldspars.

Next, special considerations for different clay bodies are explained.

Terra Cotta

This clay contains iron oxide, a colorant that's also a flux, which lowers the temperature threshold for melting a clay body. The more iron oxide, the lower the firing range of a clay body.

White Earthenware

This clay body is more complex, since its composition depends on how it is prepared. (It is not found in natural formations.) The main flux is talc or frit. White earthenware is a low-temperature clay body.

Stoneware

The main flux in stoneware is feldspar. There are two types of stoneware: mid range and high fire, depending on the formulation of the clay body.

Porcelain

The flux for this clay body is also feldspar. Porcelain behaves similarly to stoneware, but because it contains more flux, it can warp or deform more easily.

◄ ▼ When terra cotta is fired too hot, it forms craters. Then, as the temperature continues to increase, it will completely melt.

◄ ▼ Note what has happened to these two sculptures by Joan Serra when they were fired beyond their temperature range. These forms, which appear to be ruined, are very interesting from an artistic point of view.

▶ This sculpture by Joan Serra demonstrates what happens when clays with different firing ranges are mixed: some melt, and others remain intact.

CLAY BODY TEMPERATURES		
Clay Bodies	Approximate Firing Range	Approximate Melting Temperature
Terra Cotta	1760°F–1886°F (960°C–1030°C)	1922°F–2012°F (1050°C–1100°C)
Earthenware	1760°F–1922°F (960°C–1050°C)	1976°F–2102°F (1080°C–1150°C)
Stoneware	2192°F–2372°F (1200°C–1300°C)	2417°F–2462°F (1325°C–1350°C)
Porcelain	2192°F–2372°F (1200°C–1300°C)	2417°F–2462°F (1325°C–1350°C)

When subjected to heat, clays give off water and slowly transform into a vitreous body.

The firing of ceramics doesn't merely consist of bringing the kiln up to a specific temperature. The heating and cooling cycles are very important, and they must be carried out at a specific rate of speed.

As the temperature rises during the firing, the kiln will go through the following phases:

Water Smoking

The first phase of firing occurs between room temperature and around 428°F (220°C). This is the drying process, and it removes the physical water. During this phase, it's a good idea to keep the door of the kiln slightly open in order to let the steam out. This eliminates moisture on the walls of the kiln and prevents oxidation of the panels. The length of time for this stage depends on the thickness of the work, the degree of dryness, and how full the kiln is, although the average duration is about eight hours. If the piece is very thick, or if it was not dried properly and the firing is fast, it may explode because there's too much moisture inside it. If the forms are very thick or were not dried thoroughly, the time needs to be extended three or four more hours.

Chemical Water Removal

The second phase occurs between 572°F and 1292°F (300°C and 700°C). This is the process during which chemical water is eliminated from the clay body. It is also the period during which the organic materials containing carbon start to burn out.

Quartz Inversion

The third phase is known as quartz inversion. This occurs between 842°F and 1112°F (450°C and 600°C). With the temperature increase, the quartz undergoes a chemical transformation and changes from alpha quartz to beta quartz. This expansion causes an increase in volume. If the temperature rises too quickly, the pieces can break. It is recommended that the kiln be fired slowly through quartz inversion.

▲ In the fourth phase of the firing process, the kiln is between 1112°F and 1872°F (600°C and 1022°C).

▶ At the lower temperature levels, the kiln can be cooled by opening the door just slightly.

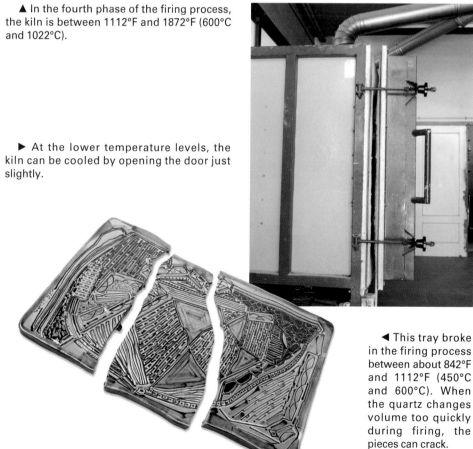

◀ This tray broke in the firing process between about 842°F and 1112°F (450°C and 600°C). When the quartz changes volume too quickly during firing, the pieces can crack.

Final Phase

In the fourth and final phase of firing, which occurs between 1112°F and 1872°F (600°C and 1022°C), the potter merely needs to observe the cones to determine when the firing is complete. The length of the firing may vary depending on the thickness of the pieces and how full the kiln is.

A medium load of work of a normal thickness, firing to a temperature of 1872°F (1022°C), will take about eight hours. The heavier the work and the greater the load in the kiln, the longer the firing will last.

▼ Teresa Gironès, figure from the Las Meninas series. Slab built, fired at high temperature. Pieces of considerable size and with thick walls must be fired slowly.

Kiln Atmospheres

The type of atmosphere in the kiln is very important. It is important to have an oxidation atmosphere during the period when the water and gases are released from the clay. There are three atmospheres that can be used in combustion kilns: oxidation, reduction, and a neutral atmosphere. The atmosphere used will produce distinctly different results.

Oxidation

An oxidation atmosphere is produced inside a kiln when there is an excess of oxygen. Bisque firings and many glaze firings are done in an oxidation atmosphere.

Reduction

A reduction atmosphere is produced inside a kiln when there is a deficit of oxygen. If there is not adequate oxygen during combustion, carbon dioxide and carbon monoxide are produced. If this occurs in a closed kiln, the carbon monoxide tries to obtain oxygen from the nearest source—in this case,

◄ When loading the kiln, the speed of the firing must be considered; the bigger the load, the slower the firing.

the work in the kiln. The clay and the glaze will be chemically altered and will change color. This change due to the loss of oxygen is referred to as reduction. A reducing atmosphere is easy to produce in any combustion kiln (gas, wood, oil, etc.). The most spectacular results are obtained with copper oxide, which produces reds, and with iron oxide, which produces bluish greens.

Cooling

To achieve proper cooling of the fired work, the physical and chemical transformations related to the process must be considered. Thus, because the quartz inversion phase creates a considerable change in volume, the cooling must be very slow. Excessively rapid cooling causes major contraction throughout the piece, which may produce tensions and cracking, either right away or days after it is removed from the kiln.

The speed of cooling, whether in oxidation or in reduction firing, will affect the final appearance of the work. Cooling should always be slow and controlled, especially during quartz inversion.

◄ This decorative piece was oxidation fired. The low-temperature glaze is composed of the following: lead frit (lead bisilicate) 70 percent, silica 30 percent, and chromium oxide 0.5 to 5 percent. Several shades of red were created during the oxidation firing to 1652°F (900°C).

▼ Glaze samples. The recipe is 34 g sodium feldspar, 36 g silica, 15 g whiting, 12 g borax, 2 g tin oxide, 1 g kaolin, and 1 g copper carbonate. Reduction fired to 2300°F (1260°C)

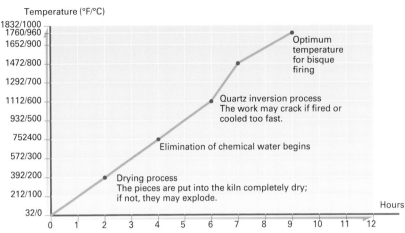

Firing Curve for Bisque Ware

Temperature (°F/°C)

1832/1000
1760/960
1652/900
1472/800
1292/700
1112/600
932/500
752400
572/300
392/200
212/100
32/0

Optimum temperature for bisque firing

Quartz inversion process
The work may crack if fired or cooled too fast.

Elimination of chemical water begins

Drying process
The pieces are put into the kiln completely dry; if not, they may explode.

Hours
0 1 2 3 4 5 6 7 8 9 10 11 12

▲ Many colors can be produced in an oxidizing atmosphere.

Firing Curve for Mid-Ranged Glazed Ware

Temperature (°F/°C)

2012/1100
1832/1000
1652/900
1472/800
1292/700
1112/600
932/500
752400
572/300
392/200
212/100
32/0

Optimum temperature for bisque firing

Vitrification process and melting of glaze

Quartz inversion process
The work may crack if fired or cooled too fast.

Water removal

Hours
0 1 2 3 4 5 6 7 8 9 10 11 12

◄ Color obtained using a glaze containing copper oxide in a reduction firing to 2300°F (1260°C)

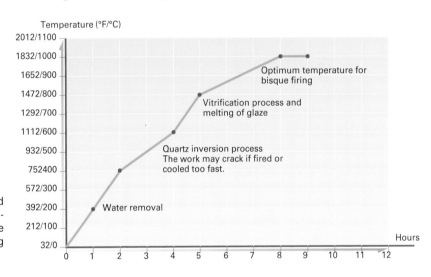

Firing Curve for High-Temperature Glazed Ware

Temperature (°F/°C)

2372/1300
2192/1200
2012/1100
1832/1000
1652/900
1472/800
1292/700
1112/600
932/500
752400
572/300
392/200
212/100
32/0

Variable completion of firing depending on the type of clay body

Vitrification process and melting of glaze

Quartz inversion process.
The work may crack if fired or cooled too fast.

Hours
0 1 2 3 4 5 6 7 8 9 10 11 12

► Joan Carrillo, Vessel. Slab built, luster fired in reduction to 1872°F (1022°C)

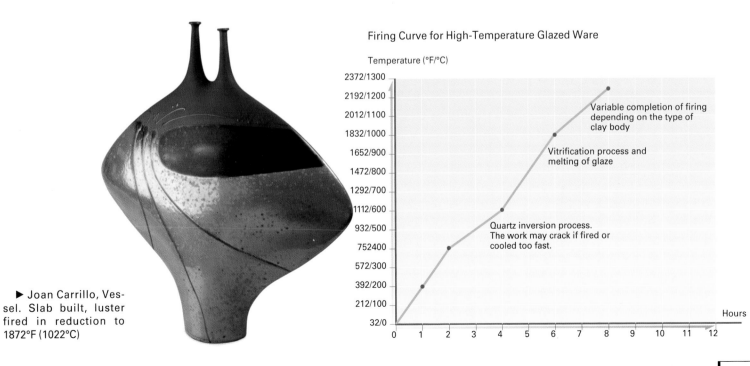

*H*and building, wheel throwing, and mold production are the most important and common processes used in making ceramics. They have been used since the dawn of humanity to produce ceramic vessels. Before making any shape, a ceramist needs to address several issues that relate to the desired results, for all of these have an effect on the production method to be used: shape, size, firing temperature range, and the clay body to be used.

For working on complex shapes, hand building is advised. The most commonly used hand-building processes presented in this chapter include pinching and coil building. Slab building and working with solid pieces of clay, as well as mold work and throwing, will also be considered.

Production
Processes

Hand Building and Throwing

The techniques presented here are the basic ones, but they can be altered in a number of ways to fit personal aesthetics. Perhaps the most difficult part of the entire process is deciding which technique is most suitable for each project. Choosing the most appropriate technique sometimes requires years of experience.

One of the best-known methods adapted to a broad spectrum of work is coil building. This was the ancient method used to make bowls and vessels. It can be used, however, to create sculptures as well.

The pinch method is the best choice for small objects, such as cups and small bowls. The shapes sometimes come out a little rough and uneven, but they bear the unmistakable mark of having been worked entirely by hand. Slab building is a technique that can be used to make large sculpture; this technique will be presented later.

When it's necessary to produce a specific number of pieces in a short time, the best technique is throwing on the potter's wheel.

◄ Carlets, Sculpture. Various slab techniques. This form illustrates the many possibilities of hand building.

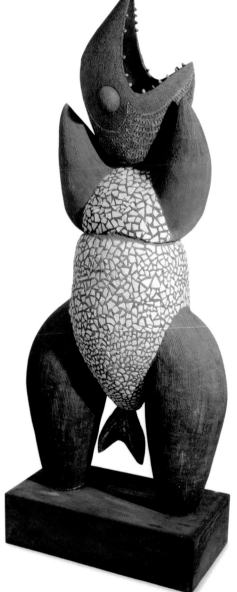

► Núria F., Sculpture. Assembled from solid and hollowed-out clay

Hand building, though, is unique. For anyone who takes a piece of clay in hand for the first time, it's an emotional experience to create and to allow creativity and freedom of expression to flow.

Everyone has a creative streak; however, some people don't develop it or even attempt to discover it. There is no age limit for discovering your creativity and allowing it to blossom.

◄ Mercè Coma, Sculpture. Slab built, fired at high temperature, with mixed-media additions

To begin, all that is required is a ball of clay and your fingers. This method is suitable for making small pieces. Very plastic clays that are properly wedged and moist enough to allow pinching, but not so moist that they collapse while being worked, should be used.

Form a ball of clay the size of a large orange and hold it in one hand while you work with it. Push straight down toward the center of the ball with your thumb. Still using your thumb, work from the center toward the outside, and keep pushing out and up as the cavity deepens. Turn the ball of clay slowly while pressing gently into the center with your thumb. Continue turning and pressing the clay. The rotation must be slow in order to create uniform pressure and a wall of consistent thickness. When the piece is finished, it is allowed to dry before firing.

► Pinched bowl made from pyritic stoneware (iron pyrite blended into stoneware clay)

▼ Ivet Bazaco, floating bowls with candles, arranged in a pond

◄ 1. It is very easy to make a bowl by pinching. Place a ball of clay in one hand and use the thumb of the other hand to push a hole in the center of the ball. Press out on the interior walls of the clay ball with the thumb, and press in with the fingers on the wall's exterior to keep the shape from distorting.

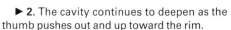

► 2. The cavity continues to deepen as the thumb pushes out and up toward the rim.
Once the pinching is finished, place the piece upside down and smooth it very slowly with a rib. Once the surface is smooth, go over it with a damp sponge.

◄ 3. To make the foot, mark the circumference and score the clay with a needle tool. Place a coil of clay on the scored surface.

► 4. Finish by using a wooden modeling tool to shape and perfect the foot. Smooth the base with a damp sponge.

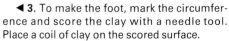

Coil Building

The coil-building technique requires a very workable clay. Coil-built forms should be constructed on a support that turns or on a banding wheel so the object can be worked easily on all sides. Clay's ability to keep its shape makes it well suited to any type of sculpture. In the case of large, thick pieces, the clay should contain 20 to 30 percent grog, which makes it more porous and less subject to shrinkage, thereby preventing breakage during drying and firing. Sculptures should be built hollow from coils or slabs, or they should be hollowed out once they are built because when the kiln temperature reaches the point at which the physical water is released from the clay, solid pieces may explode.

▲ Maria Picanyol, Large sculptures. Coil built, with cuts

▶ Before starting any project, ceramists can make a small sketch to serve as a guide during the construction process. It can be difficult to achieve satisfactory results without thinking about the work in advance.

▶ 1. Various shapes can be used to form the base of a piece. The slab roller can be used to control the thickness.

▶ 2. If you don't own a slab roller, you can use a wooden roller, along with a canvas cloth and two wooden sticks of the desired thickness.

▲ 3. To make a round slab, place the clay on the banding wheel and rotate the wheel while holding a cutting tool steadily against it. It's important to keep your cutting arm very rigid.

▲ 4. This slab is the base of the piece. Score the outer edges of the slab where the first coil will be placed. Slip is used to "glue" clay pieces together. It is applied to the scored area, and the first coil is placed on the slipped area to begin building up the piece.

▲ 5. Thicker coils must be used for large works. Use the palms of the hands to roll the coil against the table while simultaneously sliding the hands back and forth from the center toward the two ends.

▶ **6.** After the coil is a uniform thickness of just over ¹/2 inch (1.5 cm), place it onto the slab along the scored outer edge. Cut the ends of the coil at an angle and connect them. The best way to attach the coil to the base is to use the fingers; however, if the clay is stiff, a wooden modeling tool can also be used.

▶ ▶ **7.** Using your fingers to attach the coils also makes it possible to shape the piece more effectively as the walls continue to rise.

▶ **8.** After every four to five coils, smooth the walls with a rib and make sure that the evolving shape is in keeping with the design. This time also allows the clay to firm up. If you have to stop working for several hours, cover the form with a piece of plastic to keep it moist. Upon resuming work, score the clay and moisten it again

◀ **9.** The coils are leveled from time to time to prevent the work from rising unevenly. Also check the measurement of the opening to keep track of when to change the direction of the coils.

▶ **10.** Once the desired shape is established and the surface smoothed, the piece can be enhanced by using a round trimming tool to create decorative relief around the base while slowly rotating the banding wheel. A trimming tool with a larger loop is used to produce the convex groove. Tools can be chosen based on specific needs.

▶ **11.** When the piece is nearly dry, smooth the grooves with steel wool. Smooth the entire piece in the same way and allow it to dry until it's ready to be fired.

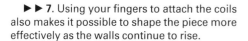

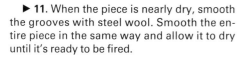

▲ **12.** The finished form with low-fire glaze, by Ivet Bazaco

Slump Molds

Working with slabs offers an endless array of possibilities. With slump molds, curved or irregular shapes can be created by fitting the slabs to a previously constructed form and using that form as a mold, whether it be a plate, a bowl, a bottle, or some other item.

In this case, a standard round plate with three feet was used as a slump mold. Since the plate is a bisque-fired piece with a porous surface that reacts like plaster, the clay can be placed in direct contact with it. The bisqued plate absorbs the water; therefore, the clay will not stick to the plate's surface. When working on a nonporous surface such as glass or plastic, it's necessary to use a cloth or thin plastic to avoid direct contact; otherwise, the clay will stick, making it difficult to remove the slab without cracking.

The best molds are made from plaster; they absorb the moisture from clay very well so that the piece firms up quickly and is ready for trimming. Molds made from bisque ware also work well. On the other hand, if a plastic mold is used, it may take two or three days for the finished work to dry.

► This work was made by Claudi Casanovas with a slump mold, using clays with different firing ranges.

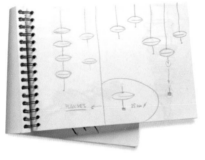

▲ These decorative serving trays were made by Roser Oliver, using slump molds.

◄ The design notebook should always be present in the studio.

▲ **1.** Any object found in the studio can be used as a mold. A slab of clay is placed inside the mold and fitted to its shape.

▲ **2.** Any cutting tool can be used to cut the slab to the correct dimensions. This is done when the clay is leather hard; that is, when it's hard but not bone dry.

► **3.** Any cutting tool can be used to cut the slab to the correct dimensions. This is done when the clay is leather hard; that is, when it's hard but not bone dry.

▲ **4.** The edges of both halves are scored and brushed with slip. This is the best way to join two moist surfaces. If one piece becomes too dry, mix up some powdered clay diluted with vinegar and use this as the slip.

▲ **5.** Join the two pieces while they are still in the molds and press them together gently to attach them. Both surfaces must be of the same wetness; if they're not, some cracks may result.

▲ **6.** Next, use the molds to press one half against the other. Doing this prevents warping, since the clay retains the shape of the mold. Leave them in the molds for four hours, until the molds absorb the moisture and the clay stiffens up.

◄ **7.** Remove one of the two molds and support the exposed clay with the other mold while smoothing the clay surface. With curved pieces such as this one, always leave one side supported inside the mold to prevent distortion.

▶ **8.** Because this is a completely closed shape, a round metal tool is used to make a hole in both the bottom and top halves to allow air to escape as the piece dries. In this case, a soup bowl was used as a base so the tool could come out the other side more easily, ensuring that the two holes would line up perfectly.

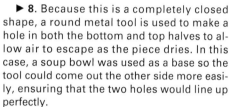

◄ **9.** This installation is composed of several identical pieces mounted with metal wire. They are hung in a large space for effect.

▶ In this slab-built sculpture by Joan Serra, the cracks serve as decorative effects.

Mold Production

This chapter will explain the process of making ceramics with molds. It will cover the modeling, the reproduction, the waste mold, and the casting mold. In addition, an introduction to wheel molds and jiggering is included. This is a complex area of ceramics, but people who devote enough time to mold making can become quite skilled.

Molds

Making work with molds is a multistep process that makes it possible to create identical pieces perfectly and very quickly by using plaster molds. The use of molds goes back to the most ancient civilizations (Mesopotamian, Egyptian, Roman, Arabian, and others), in which people used fired clay molds to create pressed decorations. Plaster is one of the most commonly used materials for making molds. Its properties make plaster a very practical material that has many applications in ceramics production. Ceramists commonly use it for its ability to imprint the finest details in a piece, as well as for its water absorption capability, the ability of its pores to remain open, and its low cost. It is often used for making slabs to reclaim and recycle clay. However, working with it is slow and complicated.

In fact, artists often ask professional mold makers to create the original mold, which the artists can then use to make identical works in quantity. Ceramists can also purchase ready-made molds from ceramics suppliers, which they can then use to make multiples.

There are a great variety of molds, which are divided into two main groups: press molds and casting molds. *Press molds* can consist of anything from simple, hand-packed molds to more complex industrial molds.

Casting molds are those that hold slip to produce the piece. The mold is filled with slip, and the plaster absorbs some of the moisture from the clay, the outer layer of which stiffens. Then the mold is emptied of excess slip and placed upside down. When the clay becomes leather hard, the mold is opened and the piece is removed.

Plaster

Molds are made with pottery plaster, which is derived from gypsum ($CaSO_4 \cdot 2H_2O$). A dehydration process is used to produce plaster ($CaSO_4 \cdot 0.5H_2O$). There are many types of plaster to choose from.

► Press molds, along with the form made in these molds

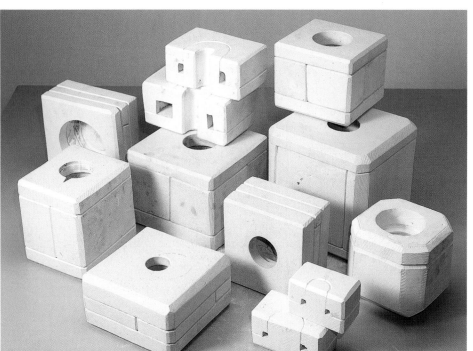

◄ A series of molds ready for use

Before making any molds, it's important to know what plaster will be used in the work. Many types of plaster are available—they are offered in different qualities designated by number, and they have various uses in such disparate fields as ceramics, construction, dentistry, and industrial ceramics. Their characteristics and properties vary from one to another. The fact that some plasters harden or shrink more than others increases or decreases the mold time. Two plasters commonly used are Ceramical and Pottery Plaster #1. Ceramical is very dense; it is extremely hard and doesn't absorb much water. It is used for dies, press molds, and very detailed molds, since it produces a perfect finish. The mix is prepared using approximately three parts plaster to two parts water.

Pottery Plaster #1 has a great capacity for water absorption. It is used for high-production casting and molds for wheel production. The mixture is prepared using approximately three parts plaster to two parts water.

Once clays used to make molds become contaminated with plaster, they cannot be reused. Plaster is a calcium sulfate, and as such, when it comes into contact with the moisture in the environment after firing, it absorbs water and expands. As a result, it exerts pressure that chips the bisque and leaves a hole with a white tip, which ruins the surface.

Most plasters harden about 20 to 30 minutes after they come into contact with water. The process can be accelerated by vigorous hand stirring, working with hot water instead of cold, or using an electric mixer. On the other hand, to slow down the process, simply add small amounts of vinegar, acetic acid, or boric acid.

PLASTER MIXTURES FOR MOLD MAKING	
Press mold	Ceramical
Die	3 parts ceramical + 2 parts #1
Model	2 parts ceramical + 3 parts #1
Press mold	1 part ceramical + 5 parts #1
Slip-casting mold	#1
Wheel mold	#1

◄ Antònia Roig, Bowl with fountain. Mold made, glazed, fired at high temperature

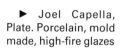

► Joel Capella, Plate. Porcelain, mold made, high-fire glazes

► Joel Capella, Sculpture. Porcelain, mold made. Large porcelain pieces can only be made in a mold; otherwise, they experience severe tension and warping.

Preparing the Plaster

When you buy plaster, it's a good idea to get only the amount you need because once the bag has been opened, the plaster absorbs moisture and will be ruined. The bag must be stored in a dry place, preferably without touching the ground.

▼ **2.** Pour clean water into a rubber or plastic bucket. Add the plaster to the water—never the other way around—continuously and evenly, sprinkling it in slowly to avoid forming lumps.

► **1.** Prepare to mix the necessary amount of plaster and water.

▲ **3.** It's very important that the plaster be absorbed into the water. When all the dry plaster is added and totally moist, let it sit for a few minutes.

▲ **4.** With your hand submerged to the bottom of the bucket, stir smoothly in circles, always in the same direction, so that any air bubbles come to the surface. Do not add any more water or plaster.

◄ **5.** When you can feel resistance, stop stirring. Strike the base of the bucket to allow any air bubbles to rise to the surface.

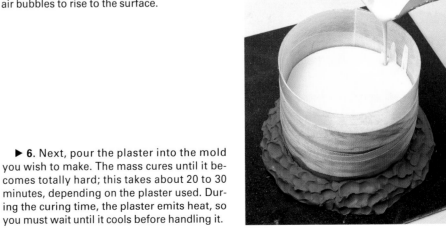

► **6.** Next, pour the plaster into the mold you wish to make. The mass cures until it becomes totally hard; this takes about 20 to 30 minutes, depending on the plaster used. During the curing time, the plaster emits heat, so you must wait until it cools before handling it.

Deflocculants

Deflocculants are materials that are added to slip to assist in particle suspension. The two deflocculants most commonly used are sodium carbonate and sodium silicate. The required quantities can vary from 0.2% to 0.5% of the dry clay weight, which is determined in large part by the physical quality of the clays. It's not possible to establish fixed rules or methods for preparing a good slip for casting. A clay body is a variable material; not only is every clay different, but the same clay in combination with other raw minerals, especially water, undergoes continual variations. It's necessary to produce a slip with the right suspension and casting qualities with the least amount of water. Following are the approximate quantities of water for each clay:

- Sculptural clays, 16% to 18%
- Stoneware, 20% to 22%
- Earthenware, 23% to 28%
- Vitreous porcelain, 23% to 28%
- Hard porcelain, 28% to 30%

So, for example, a formula for earthenware may contain 11 pounds (5 kg) of powdered earthenware clay body, 2 quarts (1.9 liters) of water, 0.18 ounce (5 g) of sodium carbonate, and 3.38 fluid ounces (101 mL) of sodium silicate. The clay body is prepared in the following way:

▶ **1.** To start, select and weigh each material.

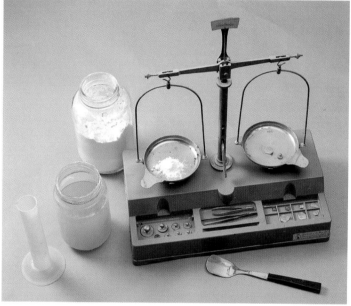

▶ **2.** The sodium carbonate and the sodium silicate require a little more precision because such small quantities are involved. Precision scales are used.

▶ **3.** After the materials are weighed, they can be mixed together. The clay is slowly sprinkled into the water in order to avoid creating lumps.

▶ **4.** Once the clay is mixed with the remaining materials, they are stirred by hand or with a household mixer or a rubber spatula until smooth.

Mold Soap

To keep the plaster from sticking to another surface, a release agent is applied. In this case, a mold soap in gel form is used. To prepare the soap, about 1 pound (.5 kg) of mold soap is placed in a metal container, and 1 or 2 quarts (.9 or 1.8 liters) of water are added, depending on the desired gel consistency, until the soap is thoroughly dissolved. Heat the mixture to boiling. Let it cool, then apply it with a brush to the entire surface of the mold.

▼ This molded form from the Rogenca studio is a bit complicated, since the lid requires a separate mold.

▲ When making mold soap, a small burner is needed to heat the mixture.

Model

A model of the form to be reproduced is made, and the first mold is made from this model. The model is almost always destroyed upon opening the mold, especially if the model is made of clay; it has to be removed from the inside of the mold, and it normally breaks during this process.

The models for these molds are commonly made of clay, and two layers of plaster are poured over them. The first layer is tinted with a color, and the second is white. The tinted layer serves as a warning: it indicates that the reproduced model is just beneath the plaster surface. As the mold is broken apart and the tinted layer is reached, that layer must be removed very delicately.

These molds are the best system for producing a plaster model, given the material's great homogeneity and the ease of producing good results, even with detailed forms.

If the original model is round, it's better to produce it by turning a block of plaster to the approximate shape and final measurements after it has stiffened but is still workable, then altering and smoothing it once it's cured.

▲ A plaster mold can be made of this small clay sculpture by Salvi Ros. This is the model, which is also called the original. It will be destroyed in the mold-making process.

Waste mold refers to the mold used to make a single reproduction of the plaster model. It is used as an intermediate step to produce a solid reproduction of a modeled piece. These molds are made up of one or more pieces, depending on their complexity. A prototype is modeled from any type of clay or other material, which may end up being totally destroyed.

Another mold is then made for production, so it's best to use clay figures that are easy to remove and that make it easy to release the material from the mold.

The form made as a model is a small sculpture. Because of its complexity, the final mold (see pages 63–64) will be made in three parts.

▶ **1.** Place the sculpture onto a flat surface and surround it with a thick coil of clay, placed about 1 to 1 ¹/₂ inches (2 to 3 cm) away from it to contain the freshly prepared liquid plaster once it's poured.

▶ **2.** Cover the model with a thin layer of plaster tinted with any kind of stain. This makes it easier to distinguish the model from the mold at the end of the process.

▶▶ **3.** When the plaster has stiffened, remove the clay coil and place boards around the piece to create a box with about 1 ¹/₂ inches (3 cm) of clearance.

▼ **4.** Next, prepare the white plaster and fill the box to a depth of a little more than 1 inch (2.5 cm) above the model

◀ **5.** Once the box is full, give a few gentle taps to the boards with a rubber mallet to allow any air bubbles to rise. Once the plaster cools, remove the boards, turn the mold over, and remove the model from inside the mold. Note the two colors of plaster.

▼ **6.** Once the mold is empty, clean the interior with a sponge and water.

► **7.** Apply several coats of mold soap gel to the inside of the mold to act as a release agent. This waterproofs the surface and prevents the plaster (poured in the next step) from sticking to it. It's important to ensure that once the interior surface of the mold is coated, there are no lumps or bubbles left, for that would affect the reproduction.

► **8.** As the plaster is slowly poured into the mold, the mold is tapped repeatedly with a rubber mallet to eliminate air pockets.

▲ **9.** Once the plaster has cured, the mold is turned over and cut apart. A saw is used to make two cuts in the shape of a cross, each a little less than 1 inch (2 cm) deep.

▲ **10.** Next, a chisel and two thin metal tools are used to form a wedge; they are struck with a mallet or hammer.

► **11.** The mold should break into four pieces. Once the original plaster model is complete, it can be used to make a three-part production mold.

Generally speaking, the mold is a negative of the form to be reproduced. A press mold is used to make a few reproductions or to make samples that subsequently are used as originals for making a die. The most appropriate mold system is selected for each specific purpose. The shape and the characteristics of the original will determine whether the mold should be made from one, two, or more parts. The number of reproductions needed and the type of clay to be used must also be taken into consideration. When the model is very complex, it's necessary to construct a multisectional mold. This system can be used to reproduce any design, mural, or form to complement larger works.

To construct the mold, the original model must be made in clay or plaster. Although the plaster model has been produced through the waste mold process, we will use a clay model to make the multisectional mold.

When the figure to be reproduced is complex, the mold must be made in two or more parts, ensuring that there are no undercuts that would bind the model to the mold.

► **1.** The profile of the original model is marked to define and divide the number of parts in which the mold should be made.

◄ **2.** The dividing lines are used to indicate the number of sections to be made. The model is covered with a layer of talcum powder to keep it from sticking to the bed of clay used to construct the mold. It is then placed on this bed of clay and filled up to the first dividing line.

▲ **3.** Next, two boards are set up for assembling the mold, and a putty knife or similar tool is used to smooth the clay support.

▲ **4.** The remaining boards are installed to form a box around the mold, and the outer corners are sealed with clay. The boards are held in place with clamps, and plaster is poured over the piece to a depth of about 1 to 1 1/2 inches (3 to 4 cm).

◄ **5.** Once the plaster has set, it's allowed to cool. Then the boards are removed and the mass is turned over to remove the bed of clay. Two registration keys are cut in the plaster with a rounded tool; these will help to align the two halves of the mold.

▼ **6.** After coating the model and the mold with mold soap, the four boards are put back into place. One of the two remaining parts is covered with clay (following the dividing lines) and the box is again filled with plaster. Once the plaster has set up, the boards and the clay are removed, and two more registration keys are cut. The boards and the clamps are put back into place and the entire surface is covered with mold soap.

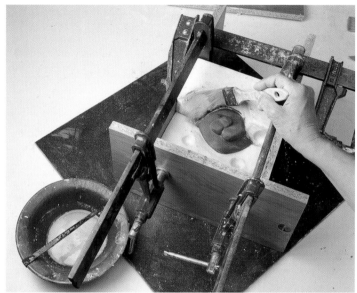

◄ **7.** The plaster is poured in at one corner to keep bubbles from forming. After the plaster has hardened, the boards are removed, the outside walls are smoothed, and a square is used to mark off the corners.

► **8.** With the mold clamped together, the largest portions are cut off with a saw. This produces a mold that's lighter and easier to handle. The smallest corners are reduced with a rasp, which is the quickest way to work. The mold is finished, and the parts are held together with large rubber bands.

Plaster Molds on the Wheel

When a specific number of identical, round pieces is desired, the model can be made of plaster directly on the wheel. This technique is done on a special wheel for plaster, which is similar to an electric potter's wheel. If you don't have this type of wheel, you can adapt the potter's wheel in your studio. Electric wheels work very well because their speed can be adjusted—an essential characteristic for turning plaster. Still, mold making is no easy task, and it requires a lengthy learning process.

◄ **1.** This exercise is performed on an electric potter's wheel. First, the splash pan of the wheel is filled with clay to the bottom of the wheel head.

▶ **2.** A sheet of fiberglass is mounted in the clay around the wheel head to act as a cylindrical container. Both the surface of the fiberglass and the wheel head are coated with mold soap. The plaster is poured to cover the top of the wheel by 2 inches (5 cm), and it is allowed to set up.

▼ **3.** Once the plaster has set, the fiberglass is removed. Stabilizing the turning tool with the wooden arm, the slab of plaster is turned until it's even and smooth, then removed. The finished plaster slab can be attached to the wheel as often as necessary. Now that this base is finished, a plaster model of any form can be poured and turned, and a slip-cast version can then be made.

▲ **4.** To begin making the model, first place the plaster base onto the wheel head. This base is coated several times with mold soap. A cylindrical sheet of fiberglass, with a diameter about $1/2$ inch (1.5 cm) larger than the piece to be made, is placed upright on the plaster and is kept in place by placing moist clay around its base.

▶ **5.** Pour liquid plaster into the fiberglass container. After it has set but is still workable, remove the fiberglass and turn the plaster to the desired shape.

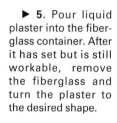

▶▶ **6.** Add a groove to serve as a grip for holding the piece. It's now ready to be cast into a mold.

Slip-Cast Mold

Slip-cast molds are made for countless items, using conventional clays or modern bodies that contain no clay.

In the slip-casting process, deflocculants are carefully added to the clay body to produce a slip with favorable suspension qualities and a minimal amount of water. Slip prepared for casting is set aside for 24 hours before being used. The first piece that comes from these molds is rarely used. Usually, the mold has to be filled three or four times for the shape to fill out completely and come out of the mold easily.

▲ **1.** The top of the plaster model (previously turned on the wheel) will become the pour hole, and the bottom will be the base. Because this model has no undercuts, a two-part mold will be made. First, locate the center of the base. Using a pencil, draw a line to divide it into two parts. The model is placed onto a slab of clay that follows the outline of the piece.

▲ **2.** The model and the boards are thoroughly coated with mold soap. These boards are placed as walls around the piece, leaving a space about 2 inches (5 cm) all around to limit the size of the mold. The model must be in a horizontal position so that one of the boards is flush with the pour hole and another is flush with the base.

▲ **3.** Once the plaster is poured, cured, and cool, the boards and the clay are removed. The mold is turned over, with the model still inside, and two notches (or keys) are cut to hold the pieces of the mold together in proper alignment.

▲ **5.** To make the second part of the mold, the boards are reassembled with clamps holding them in place, and the entire mold is thoroughly soaped. The plaster is once again poured in at one corner so that the plaster rises about 2 inches (5 cm) over the top of the model.

▶ **6.** Once the plaster has set, the boards are removed, and the two parts of the mold are held together with clamps. The notches are cut with a rounded tool. The interior of the mold is soaped, boards are reassembled with clamps, and the plaster is poured. After it hardens, it is smoothed and the corners cut off.

◀ **4.** These notches must be substantial, so they don't chip or break.

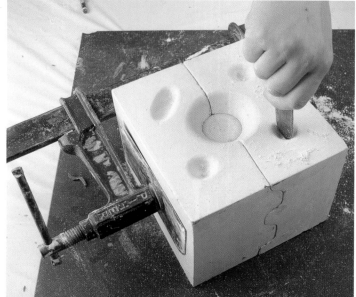

Casting from the Mold

▶ **1.** Once the mold is dry, it can be used to make reproductions. It is closed up and secured with large rubber bands. Molds can be filled with slip by using pitchers or a modern pump system. A slip that has been stored for some time generally needs to be stirred vigorously before pouring it. This can be done with an electric mixer.

▼ **2.** Once the walls of the piece have reached the proper thickness, pour the remaining slip into a bucket so it can be used again. The piece is allowed to drain inside the mold, which is placed upside down until the slip hardens and contracts slightly, at which point the mold is taken apart. There should always be extra space in the pour hole to act as a reservoir, since water from the slip is continually being absorbed into the mold. Before removing the entire piece from the mold, cut out the clay that has formed in the pour hole.

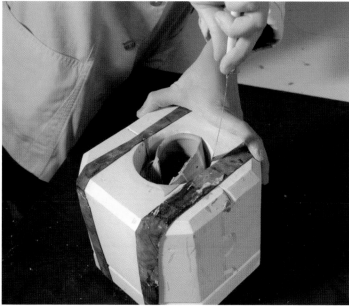

▲ **3.** Once the piece is stiff enough to retain its shape, it can be removed from the mold.

▲ **4.** During the drying process, the dividing lines from the casting are scraped and the piece is smoothed. Before the next casting, the mold is allowed to dry for a few minutes. The extra clay from the casting can be dried and recycled into slip.

▲ **5.** The completed, fired bowls. Obviously, the purpose of this process is to make a large number of pieces. It is not worthwhile to make just 50 to 100.

Making Plaster Wheel Molds

The process of forming ceramic pieces with plaster molds allows you to make both concave and convex forms. For example, it is possible to mold the inside of a plate or the outside of a bowl.

Normally, the original model is made first, then the mold is cast. Subsequent work is cast from this mold.

In this exercise, a few steps from the section on making the model on the wheel are repeated.

◄ **1.** To begin, the plaster slab made previously is placed onto the wheel head and coated with mold soap. The fiberglass wall is set on the slab to form a cylinder, and the base is secured with moist clay. Then the fiberglass cylinder is filled with about 2 inches (5 cm) of liquid potter's plaster.

▼ **2.** Before it sets up completely, the center of the plaster mass is scraped down to begin creating the general shape of the bowl's interior.

◄ **3.** The fiberglass is removed when the plaster is a bit harder so it can be shaped with turning tools. The bowl shape is finished up with a metal rib or scraper to ensure that the plaster surface is perfectly smooth. The surface can also be smoothed with fine sandpaper.

▲ **4.** In this exercise, the bowl's interior has a spiral relief. The design is marked in pencil, and a woodworker's chisel is used to carve the spiral out to the edge of the bowl.

▲ **5.** Once the design is complete, it is smoothed with sandpaper or steel wool, and the production mold can be made. The fiberglass wall is placed around the original and tied securely with rope. Clay is placed around the base of the fiberglass wall—both inside and out—to support it and to prevent plaster from leaking out. Mold soap is applied; then the plaster is poured in until the highest point of the bowl is covered by about 2 inches (5 cm). This will be the jigger mold.

Jiggering

To produce a series of objects, it's best to pour several identical production molds from the original (see the previous page) so work can continue while the jiggered pieces dry.

► **1.** After the plaster slab is attached to the wheel head, the mold can be placed on the slab. Above the wheel, the wooden profile template, attached to a pivoting arm, will help shape the clay. This technique is called jiggering, which shapes the interior and exterior of the form at the same time.

► ► **2.** A slab of clay, just under 1 inch (2 cm) thick, is cut to the desired measurement and placed on top of the mold.

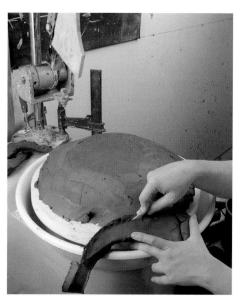

▲ **3.** Next, with the wheel in motion, the clay is pressed onto the mold using a damp sponge. Excess clay is removed with a wooden modeling tool to avoid damaging the plaster base.

▲ **4.** The wooden profile template is gradually lowered onto the clay to create the exterior of the bowl, while the pressure on the clay shapes the interior to the mold. A sponge is used to keep the clay wet and to remove excess clay.

▲ **5.** Once the surface is smooth, the work, still attached to the mold, is removed from the wheel and dried until the edges begin to come loose. It is then taken off the mold and set aside to finish drying.

◄ A bench vise is used to make the profile template, which will be mounted on the pivoting arm.

Profile Template

The profile template can be made from either metal or wood (steel is more durable). It is mounted on a lever, or pivoting arm. It is counterbalanced by a pulley and is usually fitted with a stop to prevent it from getting too close to the mold. The type of work determines the shape of the template to be used, but the shape also frequently depends on personal preference. Once the form is completely modeled, the template is raised and the wheel stopped. Then the plaster mold is removed and set aside to dry, with the clay piece still attached. The process can be repeated with another mold. The work is removed from the mold once it hardens and begins to come loose from the mold.

The production speed of this method depends on the plasticity of the clays and the size of the work. Molds made of Pottery Plaster #1 have a porosity of about 30 percent and can't be used to make more than about 300 pieces.

The Potter's Wheel

This chapter explains the basic concepts for throwing bowls, plates, cylinders, vases, and teapots on the potter's wheel.

The potter's wheel was one of the first mechanical tools developed by humans. There are many written accounts of how and where the potter's wheel originated, depending on geographical area. Today, potters can choose which wheel type they prefer to use. The progress of civilizations made it necessary to produce a great number of containers for holding food and liquids, as well as funerary urns and construction materials. Ceramics have played a decisive role in the production of these objects.

Getting Started on the Wheel

The first time you sit at a potter's wheel, it's very difficult to pay attention to the position of your body, since all of your attention is focused on your hands. However, as you improve the position of your hands, it's important to adjust the position of your body to ward off fatigue.

Sit at the wheel at the same height as the wheel head or slightly above it, and close enough to the wheel to work comfortably. Your arms need to be relaxed and held close to your sides. When your hands are on the clay, your body should lean forward. Since a great amount of pressure needs to be applied to the clay, it's important that the arms remain tight to your sides throughout; otherwise, the clay will become unstable and move off center. The hands, wrists, and arms must be held firmly and steadily, yet must be relaxed enough to feel the pressure of the hands on the clay. The left arm exerts greater pressure than the right.

▼ When working at the wheel, it is important to maintain the aesthetic lines of the shape. These vessels by Josep Maria Mariscal are very well thrown and retain the proper symmetry.

▼ These bowls by Barbaformosa demonstrate that it's possible to throw very thick pieces on the wheel.

▶ When working at the wheel, it's important to find the best and most relaxed position for your body. The arms can rest against the legs; the body leans slightly forward.

▲ The bowl is one of the first shapes that people throw on the wheel. It's important to try throwing large bowls as well because the first and second pulls provide an opportunity to practice.

▶ A potter can select the proper clay from a number of choices. A good clay possesses a high amount of plasticity and water absorption capacity, yet doesn't produce significant shrinkage in the fired piece. This category includes many varieties of clays, such as terra cotta, earthenware, and stoneware bodies. All are available from ceramics suppliers.

Throwing

When throwing, the body should be relaxed, the mind should be clear, and the potter's concentration should be solely on the sense of touch, in order to feel every rotation of the wheel and the response of the clay to the pressure from the hands. It's crucial to release the hands from the clay from time to time and to do some relaxation exercises.

At the wheel, pressure is applied to the clay at a single point. If pressure is applied to more than one spot at a time, with a finger or a part of the hand, the shape registers this pressure and could move off center. Learning to throw on the wheel demands a slow, continuous learning curve. Before starting, experiment with throwing exercises, body positions, and the physical exertion required by this method. It is also worthwhile to take classes from an experienced person before jumping into this field.

◀ Vessel, white clay body, low-fire glaze. Throwing a form such as this requires a great deal of experience.

▶ Jean-Paul Azaïs, Thin-walled vessel. Thrown, burnished, fired in reduction in a wood kiln

Wedging

It can be difficult to determine the right amount of moisture needed to keep a clay body plastic, and how to wedge the clay properly to avoid trapping air inside, which can cause cracks during drying or firing.

Some of the difficulties that ceramists encounter while throwing on the wheel are due to the lack of uniformity in the clay body. Clays to be thrown on the wheel must be wedged well beforehand. There are three reasons for this: Effective wedging homogenizes the clay, encourages plasticity, and eliminates air bubbles.

Air bubbles inside the clay can easily cause a thrown piece to move off center. They can also cause cracks in the final piece, as the clay shrinks around the air bubble. These may not be visible until after the final firing. To avoid bubbles in the clay, the only solution is to wedge it well, either by hand or with a pug mill.

◀ Claywork should be completely dry when it is time to put it in the kiln; otherwise, the piece could crack severely or explode if it's heated too fast.

◀ The wheel is not used solely to produce large forms and vases. Some potters use it to throw, among other things, additions for other pieces.

▶ This series of work by Ivet Bazaco is one example of what can be produced on a potter's wheel. They are a bit more complicated but are very interesting.

◀ There are different types and sizes of pug mills used for wedging. When it becomes necessary to work for many hours on a wheel, it's a great relief to be able to use a machine for wedging; it's much easier.

Wedging by Hand

When pug mills are not available, hand wedging works very well, and it makes the clay very workable.

If the clay is very soft and sticky, it contains too much water. It must be wedged or allowed to dry for a while on a slab of plaster before trying to use it again. On the other hand, if the clay cracks when folded over, it is too dry. To rewet, a couple of pieces of clay can be cut off with a string tool and moistened by splashing them with water. They are added back into the clay body and wedged on a smooth surface until the clay is once again soft and flexible. If the clay is too dry, this method of rehydrating the clay will not work. The clay must be completely recycled again.

▲ Divide a piece of clay, preferably a very moist one, into two parts. Stack the two and wedge them together as though kneading pizza dough.

▲ Compress and squeeze in a circular motion to forcefully redistribute the flat pieces of clay into a cone shape, which is easier to work with on the wheel.

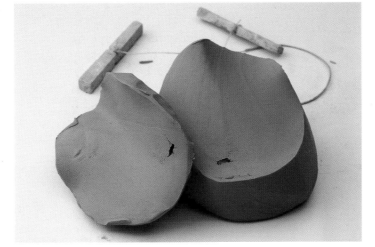

▶ After repeating this exercise many times, cut the clay through the middle to be sure that there are no bubbles in it, as there are in this example.

Preparing to Throw

Once the clay is wedged and ready for throwing, all the tools that will be used should be placed within easy reach near the wheel: a bucket of water for wetting the hands and cleaning the sponge, a wire tool, a metal rib for smoothing and shaping, a fettling knife, a small sponge, ware boards for holding the pieces that come off the wheel, and a second slop bucket for excess clay.

▶ All set to begin throwing, with the necessary tools on hand

Centering the Clay

Before throwing on the wheel, you first need to learn how to center the clay by exerting strong pressure to it. The wheel head must be dry or covered with a small amount of clay. The wheel is started in a counterclockwise direction at low speed.

▲ One step in centering involves using both hands to pull the clay up into a cone.

▲ The right hand pushes and flattens the clay. Both hands press toward the center at the same point, with equal pressure.

◄ Once the hands reach the top of the cone, they remain immobile for a few seconds without squeezing, while exerting gentle pressure with the right thumb to make sure that the clay remains completely centered. The hands are removed from the clay with great care so that it remains on center.

▶ A thrown set of bowls with added detail, from the Rogenca studio

Throwing Off the Hump

In order to make a series of identical pieces, many potters throw from the top of a large hump of clay, which is referred to as throwing off the hump. This method eliminates the need to center the clay for each piece.

▶ The hump makes it possible to work on a medium or small form. Here, the ceramist is throwing porcelain bowls.

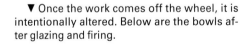

▼ Once the work comes off the wheel, it is intentionally altered. Below are the bowls after glazing and firing.

Opening the Clay

Once the clay is centered, hold your arms tightly to your sides and press both thumbs into the center of the clay to a depth of about 1 inch (2.5 cm). While doing this, support the exterior of the clay with your fingers. After making a small hole (and without removing the thumbs from the center), use the middle finger to make a small mark in the hump of clay to define the foot of the bowl or other form being made. The wrists are raised as you continue pressing the thumbs out to open the clay.

The First Pull

Place the index finger of the right hand inside the clay wall parallel to the middle finger on the outside wall. The left hand, supported by the body, supports the other side. Press out slowly with the finger, sliding the clay upward. If pressed too hard, the bowl will distort.

The Second Pull

The position of the hands changes for the second pull. The form is finished using this position. The four fingers of the left hand are placed inside the bowl, working mainly with the middle and the ring fingers, and the index finger and the thumb of the right hand are placed on the outside.

▲ **1.** The position of the hands and fingers while opening the clay

▼ **3.** The position of the hands during the second pull

▲ **2.** The position of the fingers during the first pull.

▲ **4.** This cutaway view of the bowl shows the hand positions more clearly. The fingers of the left hand are placed in a hook shape so that the middle and ring fingers do most of the pressing. Gentle pressure is applied as the clay is pulled up and thinned out. Both hands must work in parallel at all times.

▲ **5.** The surface of the bowl is smoothed by using a rib to remove excess water and clay.

▲ **6.** Finally, the rim is smoothed with a piece of damp leather (chamois).

▲ The bowl is one of the first forms thrown on the wheel by beginning ceramists. Although the decoration on this bowl is very simple, it is striking. Fired at high temperature

Throwing a Plate

In the following exercise, a plate is thrown off the hump, in a method very similar to the one used to create the bowl shown on the previous page.

◀ **1.** Once the clay is centered into a hump, both thumbs press in to open it. With your finger, make a ridge in the clay to indicate the foot of the plate.

The first pull is executed with the right hand, guiding the clay toward the potter in a flat shape, instead of pulling it upward, as when making a bowl. The left hand is used to support the piece at the edge.

▶ **2.** The second pull can be repeated two or three times depending on the size of the plate. To finish the shape and speed up production, many potters use a rib made from a section of a bisqued plate.

◀ **3.** This rib is made from a plate that was cut in half and bisque fired. It's used as a half-mold. It speeds up the production of plates of a similar or even flatter shape. When the plate is finished on the wheel, the edge is smoothed with a chamois.

▼ **4.** If it is necessary to make several plates in a short amount of time, bats can be used. These can be round pieces of wood that fit on top of the metal wheel head. The work is thrown on the bat and removed immediately. Another bat is put into place, and the process continues.

◀ Joan Carrillo, Plate. Grogged clay, thrown, with high-fire glazes. A plate is very difficult to make on the wheel, especially for beginners. Often, the shape collapses when it's nearly finished, and the process must be started all over again.

▶ This thrown vessel by Elena Montañés possesses two distinct features: the shape, with its very small foot, and the simple decoration.

Throwing a Cylinder

The cylinder is the basis for making a variety of objects—most other shapes come from it. This is a complicated technique and can take a long time to learn. It should be addressed only after several initial stages have been mastered. It's important not to move on to a new technique without first mastering the previous one.

In any throwing exercise, the clay is first centered, then opened, leaving some clay at the base of the cylinder. The base is widened by exerting pressure on the wall with the thumbs and fingers. The wall should remain at a right angle to the base.

▶ **1.** The pads of the middle and ring fingers of the left hand should be touching the interior of the cylinder, just above where the base and wall meet. The index finger of the right hand is bent into a hook shape and pressed against the exterior wall of the cylinder, at the wheel head; this finger is aided by the thumb. To keep the walls perfectly straight, press and pull up at the same time with both hands, exerting a force in proportion to the speed of the wheel.

▶ **2.** This cutaway view shows the proper hand positions.

▶ ▶ **3.** As the wall becomes taller and thinner, make several more pulls, using a rib to exert more pressure. If the lip is uneven, it can be trimmed with a needle tool while the wheel is turning.

◀ **4.** A chamois is used to smooth the lip of the cylinder. A wire tool cuts the cylinder from the wheel head.

▶ Ceramist Antònia Roig added a decorative effect to this vase by pulling out the lip a bit while throwing.

► **1.** To throw a teapot, start by making a cylinder about 6 inches high and 4 inches in diameter (15 x 10 cm). Then the body is rounded out by exerting pressure with the fingers on the interior wall. Make sure that the opening doesn't become too large. A lip can be formed with the first pull. With the left hand in position for the second pull and the right hand holding a rib, refine the shape and thin the clay near the opening.

Throwing a Teapot

For someone just beginning to throw on the wheel, making a teapot is an important goal, even though it is a complex task. Before throwing a teapot, it's helpful to draw the desired form. When considering the design, think about the following: Where will the handle attach and what will it be made of: clay, bamboo, metal, or wood? How large will the handle be, and how will it relate to the rest of the attachments? What will the spout, the lid, and the overall shape look like? There is an endless array of possibilities for alterations of this form, but these can be made only in the design phase. Once the spout or handle is attached, the teapot design is set. This is one of the few pieces thrown on the wheel that can't be made without much forethought; it must be clearly contemplated and designed in advance.

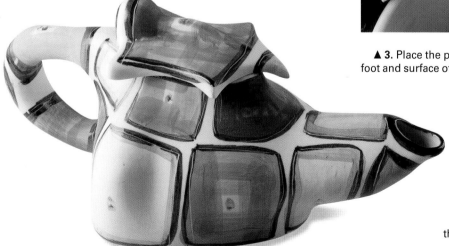

◄ **2.** Once the body of the teapot has been formed, the fit of the lid must be considered. Using the middle finger and thumb of one hand, pinch the lip while pressing down with the index finger of the other hand, making sure that the clay doesn't collapse. Let the body dry until it's leather hard.

▲ **3.** Place the piece upside down on a chuck on the wheel, then trim the foot and surface of the pot.

◄ This teapot by Montse Zurilla is a good example of the creative possibilities in throwing and altering.

Teapot Attachments

While the body of the teapot is drying, the attachments can be made: first the lid, since it has to dry before being trimmed, then the spout, and finally, the handle. While these are drying, the teapot is trimmed. Throwing off the hump is a good technique to use when making these.

The Lid

◄ To make the lid, first measure the diameter of the teapot opening. Center the clay in a cone shape for throwing off the hump, then press the thumbs into the center of the clay to open it. The first and second pulls are done as if making a saucer. Using the thumb and the middle finger of one hand, pinch the edge to create a lip, using the index finger of the other hand to press inward. The lid is cut off the hump using a wire tool and is removed to dry. Finally, it is trimmed and a knob is added.

The Spout

◄ The hump is left perfectly centered; a thumb is pressed in to open the clay, and with the first pull, a long, narrow cylinder is made. Then the base of the cylinder is widened.

► The clay is gradually and very carefully narrowed, using the middle finger and thumb on both hands to create four pressure points. Then a wire tool is used to cut off the spout and remove it from the hump. It is placed on a bat to dry before being attached to the teapot.

The Handle

► A piece of clay is shaped into a small cone.

►► Next, the cone is lengthened with the fingers, leaving one end thicker than the other. The handle is cut to size and shaped.

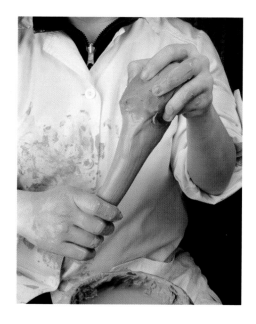

Trimming and Assembling The Teapot

There are countless ways to throw and assemble teapots, but one essential step involves trimming the body and foot. The pot is placed upside down on a chuck to be trimmed.

After the handle has been made, it is time to attach the spout.

Before attaching the spout, try it out at various angles and heights, making sure that its tip is higher than the opening of the teapot. Mark the position of the spout and use a fettling knife or other round, sharp tool to make the holes through which the liquid will flow. These holes will also serve as the tea strainer. The area on the pot is slipped, and the spout is attached. Next, when attaching the handle, secure each end to the pot carefully and reinforce them with coils of clay to strengthen the joints. If the handle is made from a different medium, the clay coils must be large and strong so they don't break after a short time.

▲ Handles made of cane or wicker are fairly easy to attach; in this case, artist Roser Milà attached the handle after the teapot was completely finished.

◄ 1. A clay chuck with an opening sized to the body of the teapot is prepared on the wheel, and the teapot is inverted and placed in it. (A cloth is laid between the two to prevent them from sticking together.) A trimming tool is used to smooth the base and trim the foot. The teapot is turned right side up and is trimmed of excess clay. Taking advantage of this position, the lid is put into place and trimmed.

▲ 2. The lid is rounded, and several incisions are made in the center of the clay to use as guides for attaching the knob. A small piece of clay is placed in the middle of the lid to form the knob, then trimmed. The lid is then set aside to dry on a bat.

▲ 3. The position of the spout must be determined. It's crucial that the tip be higher than the opening in the top of the teapot; otherwise, the liquid will run out when the teapot is filled. Make several small holes in the body of the teapot where the tea can pour out. Make sure the spout is cut to the contours of the teapot. Cut a piece of the tip off at an angle to prevent drips when pouring tea. Score and slip the pot and the spout, then attach the spout, making sure that it blends in with the body of the teapot.

▲ 4. To secure the additions to the teapot, score and slip the pot and the additions. It is also a good idea to flatten a small coil of clay around each joined area. The most appropriate handle is chosen based on the design of the teapot and is then attached. Again, the two pieces to be joined should be scored and slipped. The handle is attached and a few very small coils are added for reinforcement. Finally, a damp sponge should be used to smooth the surface of the pot; then the pot is set aside to dry.

Trimming

The piece should be thrown as close to the desired shape of the product as possible in order to cut down on the amount of trimming required.

The trimming can be done in the traditional manner: Once the form is leather hard, it is inverted and placed on a chuck that has been centered on the wheel. Using a trimming tool, remove excess clay, trim the foot, and refine the shape.

▲ **1.** To make a chuck, center the clay on the wheel, then open it to the inner diameter of the form. The chuck is covered with a very thin cloth. The form is placed upside down on the chuck and centered; then the base is smoothed with a flat metal rib.

▲ **2.** Once the base is smooth, trim the foot, and refine and shape the outer wall.

Throwing Vases

To throw a vase, begin as if throwing a cylinder. The clay is centered and opened to the floor of the piece. The right angle is marked, and the wall is raised with the second pull.

▶ **1.** When the cylinder has been pulled up to the desired height, once again both hands are used to pull up the clay, but the inside hand must move about 1/4 inch (4 mm) above the hand on the outside. The wall is thinned and the piece is given its convex shape.

▼ **2.** The hands are brought up to the rim of the piece for the first pull, and the lip is flared.

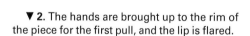

▲ Joan Carrillo, Vase. Wheel thrown, with oxides, low fired in reduction

◀ **3.** If the lip is a little off center, it is cut off with a needle tool, and its shape is refined with a rib that perfectly matches the curve of the neck of the piece.

Glaze
Techniques

Glazes are used on clay bodies that are different in both physical and chemical properties, and that also melt at different temperatures. At the same time, clays and glazes display specific properties that will vary when they are fired; thus, it's not surprising that there are a great many different recipes for glazes.

This chapter concentrates on making glazes, as well as on the composition and function of many of the raw materials that make up the glazes. Frits are used extensively for low-temperature firing, and progressively less for mid-range and high-temperature firing.

We will also briefly introduce raku glazes, copper reds, paper clay, and ash glazes.

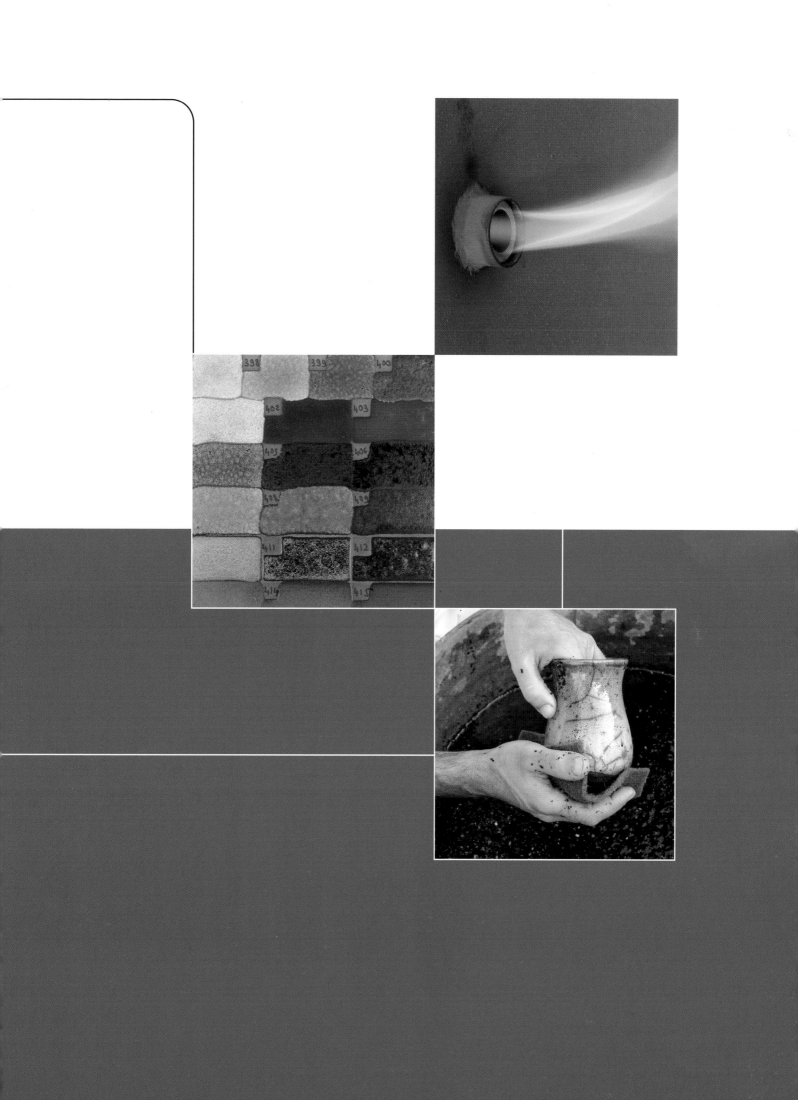

Glazes

After firing, glazes become hard and generally glossy. They are thin layers of melted glass that are applied to the surface of a pot to make it vitreous, more resistant to scratching, and smooth.

In ceramics, there is a broad vocabulary used to designate the vitreous coating on ceramic objects. These terms include glaze, cover coat, once-fired, and opaque glaze, and aside from some small differences, they are all still glazes.

Glaze. A layer of glass prepared from blends of different materials that combine evenly when they melt and attach firmly to a ceramic object. This object needs to be insoluble and impermeable to liquids and gases. In general, these glazes are transparent and provide a glossy or matte finish.

Cover Coat. A transparent glaze is applied over a slip or underglaze.

Once-Fired Glaze. This is a transparent or matte glaze that may contain color and that is usually applied to a pot that will be single fired, although it can also go through two firings.

Opaque Glaze. This glaze isn't transparent; the surface of the clay can't be seen through it.

Glaze Classifications

It's not easy to classify glazes—they present such a variety of characteristics that finding usable categories is difficult.

Glazes are classified in the following ways: First, by their firing temperature range; second, by their application; third, by their effect on the finished product; and fourth, by their chemical composition.

◄ The transparent glaze on this decorative plate by Fila-Clara is made of a leaded frit (100 g) and cobalt oxide (0.250 mg). The plate was first decorated with underglazes; then the glaze was applied. Lead glazes should never be used on functional ware.

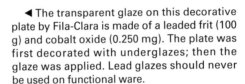

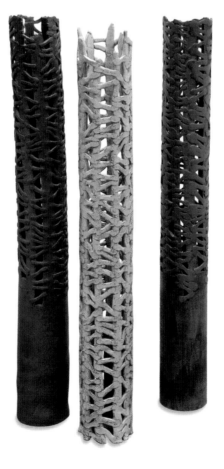

▶ These sculptures by Joan Esquerdo were surfaced with high-fire glazes. The thickness of a high-fire glaze should be about ¹/₈ to ³/₁₆ inch (3 to 4 mm)

▼ The look of the finished work depends on the glaze application. Most glazes require a thick application.

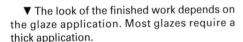

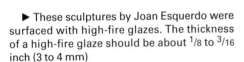

▲ These yellow kitchen tiles were coated with a transparent glaze.

▲ Michael Cleff, Slab-built sculpture, 1995. White glaze, with iron oxide applied in powder form to the top of the work

Raw Glazes

In a raw state, glaze properties are determined by the mineral content of the ingredients, the physical characteristics of the glaze itself, and especially, how well they mix with water and how finely their ingredients are ground.

Fritted Glazes

Frits are a specific blend of compounds that melt when heated. When they cool, they form a vitreous coating that is generally insoluble in water and impermeable to the gases in the kiln. The reasons for making a frit are summarized in the following five points:

Use of Water-Soluble Raw Ingredients

A frit makes it possible to use raw ingredients that are otherwise water-soluble. The water-soluble fluxes are combined with alumina and silica, heated, and then cooled and ground into a powder. Two examples are boron and alkaline frits. They're considered slightly soluble.

Reduction of the Toxicity of Various Elements

One element that used to be common in making glazes was lead oxide, which is highly toxic. Lead is soluble in acids, and if it is inhaled or ingested, it accumulates in the blood and causes lead poisoning. Fritting the lead does reduce its toxicity and solubility, but it still may cause lead poisoning. Today, it's generally not recommended for use in glazes.

Creation of Uniform Melting

A fritted glaze has added advantages when it's applied to the surface of fired clay. In producing the frit, ingredients are uniformly melted together. When applied as a glaze, they melt at a specific temperature.

Greater Stability in Glazes

When a glaze is fritted, it exhibits greater stability in the glaze firing, which makes it easier for the ceramic body and the glaze to bond together. Glaze faults may develop without the proper bonding of the glaze and clay body.

Reduction of Surface Defects

In frits, all processes of thermal decomposition are already complete; as a result, they are usually a good fit with clay bodies and underglazes. All gases are released, and there is less likelihood of pinholes, crawling, or cratering.

Making a Frit

Today, frits are essential products in the ceramics industry. They provide relatively low-cost, highly consistent materials that allow much more control in glaze formulation.

To make a frit, first weigh and mix the dry products to be fritted. Place them in the melting pot of the fritting kiln; then close and start the kiln. At a certain temperature, the materials become liquid. At this point, gases will be released, and the liquid mixture may begin to bubble violently. When the gases have been removed and the glaze stabilizes in liquid form, the drain plug is pulled from the melting pot, which allows the liquid frit to drip through the opening and to be collected in a container filled with cold water. Due to the rapid cooling, the glaze appears to have shattered into tiny particles, which are reduced to a powder in a ball mill. After grinding, it is dried to remove any remaining water. In general, to achieve thorough drying, the frit is placed in a dehydrator or inside the kiln at a temperature between 122°F and 212°F (50°C and 100°C). When the frit is dry, it is weighed; then other ingredients can be added to it. Once this is done, the fritted glazes are ready for use.

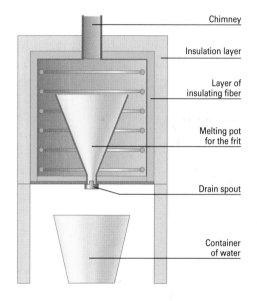

Chimney

Insulation layer

Layer of insulating fiber

Melting pot for the frit

Drain spout

Container of water

▲ A fritting kiln

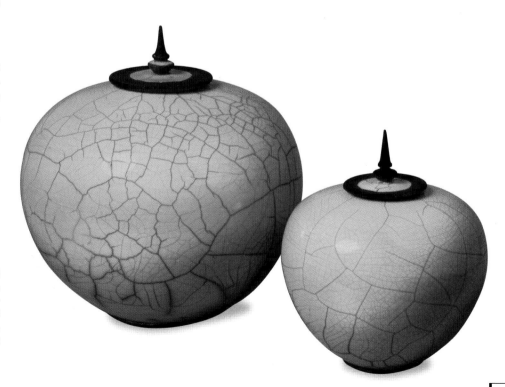

► Mieke Selleslagh, *Topot*. These vessels were decorated with a low-fire crackle glaze. The dark lines in the cracks were enhanced after firing. The surface was coated with India ink and then washed to produce this effect. The quality of the crackle depends on the glaze.

Raw Ingredients of Glazes

The glaze should make the clay surface vitreous, hard, and smooth; it may be glossy or matte, transparent or opaque. It highlights the aesthetic or decorative aspect of the work and helps adapt it to the requirements of its intended use. It is therefore important to distinguish among the various materials that are used in glazes; these are described in the following paragraphs.

Fluxes

These materials are added to a particular substance in order to lower its melting point. The most important ones are: sodium oxide (Na_2O), potassium oxide (K_2O), lithium oxide (Li_2O), calcium oxide (CaO), and boron (B_2O_3).

Glass Formers

In ceramics, these involve two items from the group of acids: silica (or silicon dioxide, SiO_2) and boric anhydride (B_2O_3).

Stabilizers

Also referred to as raw materials of the neutral group, these raise the melting point of the glaze. The main refractory material that acts as a stabilizer is alumina (Al_2O_3).

Opacifiers

These are oxides that counter the transparency of the glaze. The main oxides are tin oxide (SnO_2), zirconium oxide (ZrO_2), zirconium silicate ($ZrSiO_4$), and titanium dioxide (TiO_2).

◄ This bowl is decorated with an opaque white crackle glaze and a brushed overglaze.

► Maria Bofill, Porcelain sculpture from the *Cups* series, 1996. The upper part of the cup was decorated with a high-fire glaze containing cobalt oxide.

▲ Glazed tiles. These are fairly transparent, which allows some of the color of the clay to show through.

▲ A sample of what opaque glazes of different colors look like. The opacity completely masks the color of the clay.

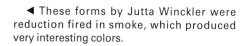

Colorants

These are divided into two large groups: oxides and stains.

Oxides

Oxides are metallic compounds of mineral origin, which can add color to a glaze without changing its transparency when mixed into the glaze. Some of the most important include copper oxide (Cu_2O), cobalt oxide (CoO_2), iron oxide (Fe_2O_3), chromium oxide (Cr_2O_3), manganese dioxide (MnO_2), and nickel oxide (NiO_2).

Stains

Commercial stains or industrial pigments (raw materials prepared by industrial mechanical processes) make up the second group. They include a broad range of colors.

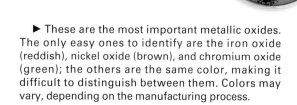

▶ These are the most important metallic oxides. The only easy ones to identify are the iron oxide (reddish), nickel oxide (brown), and chromium oxide (green); the others are the same color, making it difficult to distinguish between them. Colors may vary, depending on the manufacturing process.

◀ It's easier to distinguish between the commercial stains, since nearly all of them are the same color in the dry state as they are after the firing. Once these colors are blended with a clear glaze and fired, their colors may be even more intense than their raw color.

▼ The temperature range at which a pot will be fired must be decided before glazing the interior. Regardless of whether the interior is glazed or not, when a piece is fired between 1760°F and 1868°F (960°C and 1020°C), it will remain porous. Therefore, if the interior is to be vitreous, the work must be fired at high temperature. This vase by Antònia Roig was high fired.

◀ These forms by Jutta Winckler were reduction fired in smoke, which produced very interesting colors.

▶ This tile by Mercè Coma was decorated using *cuerda seca* (dry rope technique) and high-fire glazes.

Characteristics of Glaze Ingredients

Fluxes

▲ This interesting work doesn't need much glaze because its surface is textured.

Sodium Oxide (Na₂O)

This is one of the oxides of the alkaline group. It is a strong flux that creates bright colors. One common form used in glazes is sodium carbonate (Na_2CO_3), which is soluble in water. The melting point of sodium is 1652°F (900°C). The following compounds can be used to introduce sodium oxide into glazes: sodium feldspar ($Na_2O \cdot Al_2O_3 \cdot 6SiO_2$), nepheline syenite ($KNaO \cdot Al_2O_3 \cdot 4.6SiO_2$), sodium carbonate ($Na_2CO_3$), borax ($2B_2O_3 \cdot Na_2O \cdot 10H_2O$), or frits.

Potassium Oxide (K₂O)

This is another oxide in the alkaline group. It acts as a flux and has a strong effect on certain colorants, although not as strong as sodium oxide. Its melting point is 1382°F (750°C), and it is soluble in water, which is why it is sometimes fritted. The following materials are used to introduce potassium oxide into glazes: potash feldspar ($K_2O \cdot Al_2O_3 \cdot 7SiO_2$), nepheline syenite ($KNaO \cdot Al_2O_3 \cdot 4.6SiO_2$), or potassium carbonate (K_2CO_3).

Lithium Oxide (Li₂O)

Lithium oxide is one of the most powerful fluxes in the alkaline group. It produces a strong color response like sodium oxide or potassium oxide, but with different color effects. It begins melting around 1472°F (1800°C) and is relatively insoluble in water. The following substances can be used to introduce lithium into a glaze: lithium carbonate (Li_2CO_3), petalite ($Li_2O \cdot Al_2O_3 \cdot 8SiO_2$), or spodumene ($Li_2O \cdot Al_2O_3 \cdot 4SiO_2$).

Calcium Oxide (CaO)

This is one of the alkaline earth fluxes; the most commonly used form is calcium carbonate ($CaCO_3$). For the most part, it acts as a refractory below 2012°F (1100°C) and it contributes to opacity. The following compounds are used to add calcium oxide to a glaze: calcium carbonate ($CaCO_3$), dolomite ($CaCO_3 \cdot MgCO_3$), wollastonite ($CaO \cdot SiO_2$), gerstley borate and its substitutes, plus wood ash and bone ash.

▲ Sylvia Hyman, from the series *Sporophore and Sporophyll*, 1980. 10 inches (25 cm) in height. Porcelain slabs. A white glaze was used on the interior walls, but the exterior was left unglazed.

► Teresa Gironès, Figurative sculpture. Brushed with slips and high fired.

Lead (PbO)

This used to be an important low-fire flux, but because of its toxicity, it is used less frequently today. Its melting point is around 1616°F (880°C). While it effectively dissolves natural oxides, lead is toxic in the raw state. In an attempt to eliminate the use of lead, zinc oxide has sometimes been substituted.

Boron

All compounds that include boron oxide are water soluble, which is why they are often introduced as a frit. Boron is commonly used at low temperatures, but is used in smaller quantities at high temperatures as well. The melting point of boron is 1292°F (700°C). The raw materials that contain boron are borax, gerstley borate and its substitutes, colemanite, frits, and boric acid (H_3BO_3).

Glass Formers

Silica (SiO_2). Its melting point is around 3110°F (1710°C). It goes by many names (flint, silica, and quartz), which are generally interchangeable. Silica is a glass former; it increases hardness, durability, and acid resistance in a glaze

Stabilizers

Alumina (Al_2O_3). This is a refractory material with a melting point around 3722°F (2050°C). It is added to glazes in very small quantities and makes them opaque. When a glaze melts, the presence of alumina renders it more viscous, which prevents the glaze from running. Raw materials that introduce alumina are clays, alumina oxide, and alumina hydrate.

▶ Some sculptures don't need much glaze. Powdered iron oxide was applied to this sculpture when it was leather hard. The work, by Christos Tsimbourlas, was then reduction fired.

▶ Antònia Roig, Vessels. Stoneware, with glaze and wax resist

◀ Elena Montañés, Vessel, 1995. 8 x 11 inches (20 x 28 cm). Stoneware, with vitrified high-fire slips

▶ Fulvio Ravaioli, Vessel. Wheel thrown, with white crackle glaze

▶ In a raw state, many of the materials are difficult to identify, since many are the same color.

◀ These sample tiles are the same recipe as the one provided for the photo to the left, but the blend was colored with 10 percent colorants. The colors are much more luminous and intense.

▲ These sample tiles demonstrate the opacifying quality of titanium dioxide. This matte texture is made by blending about 6 to 10 percent titanium dioxide with a lead frit; for example, 100 g of lead frit with 5 to 10 percent titanium dioxide. Avoid adding too much chrome oxide, because it may cause cratering, as seen on tile 564 above.

Opacifiers

Tin Oxide (SnO_2)

This is an efficient opacifier of very low solubility that is added to the glaze recipe, although its high price may deter many from using it. Tin's opacifying power is very intense when added to glazes high in compounds of aluminum oxide (Al_2O_3). It deteriorates and even disappears in glazes with a high content of alkalines and boron oxide (B_2O_3). Its melting point is around 2102°F (1150°C). It is insoluble in water and highly refractory, but if fired in reduction, it loses its opacifying power and produces a gray, rough surface.

Zirconium Oxide (ZrO_2)

This is used in ceramics as an opacifier and is a basic ingredient in certain stains. The oxide acts as a refractory. The melting point is 4892°F (2700°C). The most commonly used zirconium compound is zirconium silicate ($ZrSiO_4$), which is a less refined form than the oxide. Because it contains silica, it produces glossy surfaces.

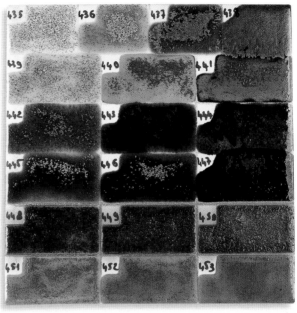

▲ Here, we can see the results of the rutile, which, compared to titanium dioxide, produces much more dramatic effects because it contains iron oxide. For these tests, rutile was blended with the frit and the six basic oxides individually (copper oxide, iron oxide, manganese dioxide, cobalt oxide, chromium oxide, and nickel oxide). The sample at the top left is the base without oxide, and the blend with each of the metallic oxides starts there.

▲ These test tiles demonstrate the effects produced by ilmenite. This mineral, when slightly ground, produces the effect of dark, fine sand in the glaze. Since it doesn't dissolve in water, it settles in certain areas. The blends on these tiles were made with the same formula as was used to produce the glazes shown on the left.

▶ This test tile demonstrates the blending effect produced by a boro-alkaline base mixed with titanium dioxide, zinc oxide, and talc, between 15 and 20 percent, plus 2 percent of each metallic oxide (see photo above left).

Titanium Dioxide (TiO$_2$)

This is available in the form of the following three minerals: brookite, anatase, and rutile. Both anatase and rutile come from ilmenite (FeTiO$_3$). White titanium dioxide is used in glazes as an opacifier. It is insoluble in water, has a high viscosity, and is refractory. The melting point is 3326°F (1830°C). It contributes very specific qualities to the surfaces of glazes, so sometimes it is used to provide texture and is considered a colorant.

Rutile (FeTiO$_3$)

This is generally referred to as light rutile or dark rutile, depending on the amount of iron present. Rutile is a mineral that contains titanium dioxide and various amounts of iron oxide. It is used mainly to modify the texture of glazes and acts as a colorant because it contains impurities, especially iron. It tends

to modify colors by contributing opacity and changes glazes to matte. It favors crystal formation in alkaline glazes rich in zinc oxide. Furthermore, it increases the surface tension and the viscosity of the glaze, raises the melting point of the glaze, modifies some colorants, and may produce mottling effects.

Ilmenite (FeTiO$_3$)

Ilmenite is black in color and coarser than rutile, and contains more than 25 percent iron oxide. It is added to glazes that are not finely ground; and in small amounts, such as one to four percent, it creates dark spots sometimes surrounded by yellow rings. In larger granulations, ilmenite darkens clay bodies and slips, gives them a mottled appearance, and adds relief.

Colorants

Vanadium Oxide (V_2O_5)

Vanadium oxide is used as an essential ingredient in a broad range of stains that run from yellow to reddish brown. It contains vanadium pentoxide mixed with a large percentage of tin oxide; a proportion of about 5 percent vanadium oxide in these stains produces a pale yellow color. If the proportion is increased to 7 to 10 percent, the result is a bold yellow that simultaneously functions as an opacifier. Vanadium oxide reduces viscosity in a melt, and it melts around 1274°F (690°C). It's highly toxic.

Manganese Dioxide (MnO_2)

In nature, this exists in the form of manganese ores, such as polianite and braunite, but can also be washed away and precipitated as a concentrated ore. Added in proportions of 2 to 4 percent, it produces brown glazes. With alkaline glazes, it may produce violets and browns. It is toxic and volatilizes at high temperatures.

Cobalt Oxide (CoO)

This can be used in the oxide form, although it's also common as a carbonate ($CoCO_3$). It is rarely encountered in its pure state. Commercially available cobalt contains around 85 percent CoO. It's one of the most popular colorants on the market because even in small amounts, it easily produces strong blue colors. Cobalt oxide produces violets when mixed with glazes containing magnesium oxide. It is toxic.

Copper (Cu)

Two popular forms in which copper can be found include copper oxide (CuO), in a blackish color, and copper carbonate ($CuCO_3$), which is green. Both forms are used in ceramics. For good dispersion in a glaze, it's better to use the carbonate because it contains less copper but has finer grains. The color of the copper depends on the firing atmosphere and the composition of the glaze.

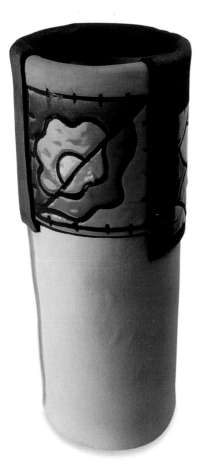

▶ Antònia Roig, Porcelain form. Stoneware glazes and decoration, fired to 2282°F (1250°C)

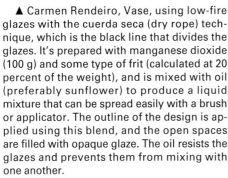

▲ Carmen Rendeiro, Vase, using low-fire glazes with the cuerda seca (dry rope) technique, which is the black line that divides the glazes. It's prepared with manganese dioxide (100 g) and some type of frit (calculated at 20 percent of the weight), and is mixed with oil (preferably sunflower) to produce a liquid mixture that can be spread easily with a brush or applicator. The outline of the design is applied using this blend, and the open spaces are filled with opaque glaze. The oil resists the glazes and prevents them from mixing with one another.

◀ Carmen Rendeiro, Plate. Low-fire glazes and *cuerda seca* (dry rope) technique

In an oxidizing atmosphere and with an alkaline glaze, turquoise colors are produced. In a reducing atmosphere at high temperature, the outcome is an intense copper red. It is toxic.

Chromium (Cr)

This material is used in glazes only as a colorant. It is found in the form of chromium oxide (CrO_2). This is a green, totally insoluble compound. At low temperatures, it colors glazes yellow, green, or reddish orange. It volatilizes around 2156°F (1180°C), so caution is needed when firing—if glazed forms containing tin oxide are located near those containing chromium oxide, there is a risk that they will flash with a pink color during firing. Chromium is toxic.

Iron (Fe)

Iron is found in various forms: red iron oxide (Fe_2O_3), black iron oxide (FeO), and yellow iron hydroxide (Fe $(OH)_3$). Iron disperses easily in glazes. The most common form of iron that is added to glazes is red iron oxide (Fe_2O_3). Its color depends mainly on the atmosphere in the kiln. In an oxidizing atmosphere, it produces yellows and browns, and in a reducing atmosphere, it creates bluish green glazes.

Nickel (Ni)

The use of nickel as a colorant depends on the composition of the glaze, the temperature, and the percentage of this metal. The colors it produces run from grayish greens to deep grays; it is not commonly used in high percentages in stains, since it tends to scum the glazes during cooling. It is added in the form of black nickel oxide (Ni_2O_3) or nickel oxide (NiO), which is gray-green. Nickel is toxic.

◄ Ivet Bazaco, Decorative form. Wheel thrown, with low-fire glazes

▲ Pep Gómez, Raku-fired vessel

◄ Mercè Coma, Sculptures. These forms demonstrate that the imagination can be used to produce very interesting work.

Other Materials

Magnesium Oxide (MgO)

Magnesium oxide is a refractory by itself. It has the highest melting point of all the oxides—around 5072°F (2800°C). The most commonly used form is the carbonate ($MgCO_3$). It is nonplastic and serves as an auxiliary flux at high temperatures. It helps opacify glazes. It acts as a refractory in low-fire glazes and causes crawling.

Some minerals and compounds that contain magnesium oxide are magnesium carbonate ($MgCO_3$), dolomite ($CaCO_3 \cdot MgCO_3$), and talc ($3MgO \cdot 4SiO_2 \cdot H2O$).

Zinc Oxide (ZnO)

Zinc oxide is a light, white powder that is extracted from the mineral sphalerite (ZnS). It is insoluble in water and nonplastic. It melts around 3587°F (1975°C), facilitates silica fusion, and encourages crystallization. It is an auxiliary flux at all temperatures, which means that it should be used in combination with another flux. If it is fired in reduction, it will change to the metal zinc (Zn) and volatilize at 1742°F (950°C). At low temperatures, it is refractory and somewhat opacifying at concentrations of 10 percent and higher. Zinc oxide and zinc vapors are toxic.

Barium Oxide (BaO)

Generally, this is a refractory material in low-fire glazes. It is added in the form of barium carbonate ($BaCO_3$). It is a very active flux in high-fire glazes and tends to produce crystallization. Some glazes containing high concentrations of barium oxide produce brilliant copper blues. In high percentages, it may produce matte or rough surfaces. It is very toxic if ingested.

▲ Prioart, Sculpture. Sculptural clays, with high-fire stains and glazes

► Maria Bofill, from the *Cups* series, 1989. Porcelain, thrown, and trimmed, with copper red oxide glaze, fired in reduction

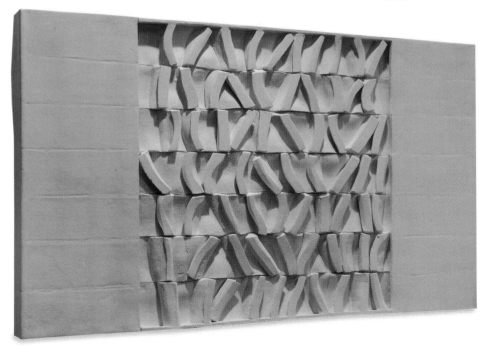

◄ Joan Esquerdo, Mural. Grogged stoneware, with white glaze. The play of shadows in this piece creates very interesting effects.

► Samuel Bayarri and Rafaela Pareja, *Water in April, Flowers in May*. Slab-built stoneware, with blue and black high-fire metallic glazes

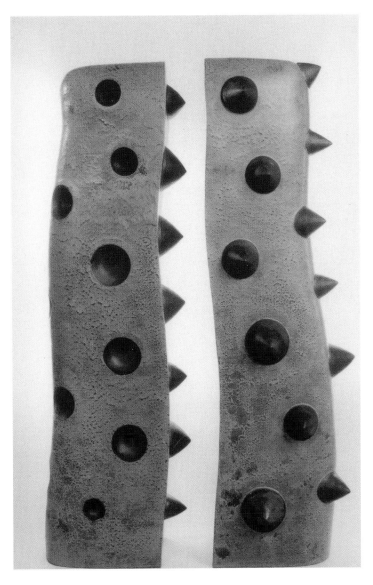

Calcium Phosphate $Ca_3(PO_4)$

This material is produced by calcining animal bones. It is a flux and an opacifier. In general, it's used in bone-china clay bodies. At high temperatures, it produces a very interesting satin-white glaze.

Kaolin $(Al_2O_3 \cdot 2SiO_2 \cdot 2H_2O)$

Kaolins are pure clays that have a set of common characteristics; for example, they are white in color, refractory, and translucent; have a broad firing range; and have low iron oxide and titanium dioxide contents in their formula. In glazes, they contribute alumina and silica. They are used to aid in suspension of a glaze and stabilize it during the firing. Too much kaolin may cause stiffness and opacity in the glaze.

▲ Mirto Maganari, Vessel. Wheel thrown, with a very fine layer of glaze, fired at high temperature

◄ This sculpture by Carlos Izquierdo was molded over a form. The clay body seems to have reached the melting point.

Low-Fire Glazes

Making low-fire glazes is relatively easy; most of the raw materials used are water-soluble or toxic, and therefore, they are primarily supplied by frit. Fritted glazes are classified as lead, boro-alkaline, alkaline, and mixed.

Lead Frits

While lead frits combine easily with most of the glaze materials and produce very luminous glazes, they are extremely toxic and should not be used on functional ware. If applying them to sculpture or decorative forms, use extreme caution.

Boron or Boro-Alkaline Frits

The melting point of these frits is 1350°F to 1920°F (732°C to 1048°C). When combined with copper oxide (CuO), they produce turquoise. If more than 14% calcium borate is used in boron glazes, it can cause crazing. To avoid this, the amounts of alumina and silica need to be increased. It's not common to use frits composed exclusively of boron. Boro-alkaline frits and alkaline-boric frits are strong melters and tend to dissolve materials such as iron oxide, titanium dioxide, magnesium carbonate, and zinc oxide, as well as some commercial stains.

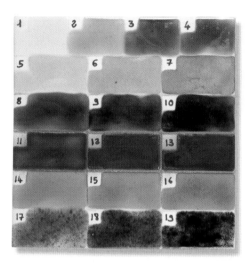
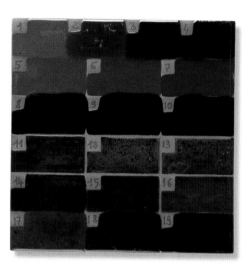

▲ Samples produced using a lead frit containing metallic oxides in the proportions of 1 percent, 3 percent, and 5 percent, arranged in columns on the tile. The top left tile is the base with no color added. These glazes were applied to a white tile and a red one; thus, their transparency is evident. The actual color of a transparent glaze can be seen only if it is applied to white or slipped clays. Use extreme caution if working with lead; do not use it on functional ware.

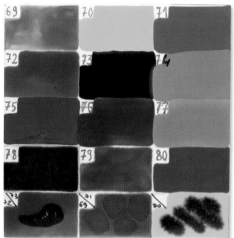

▲ Results obtained from a lead frit with commercial stains in the proportion of 15 percent. These frits considerably improve the luminosity of all colorants, especially the reds, oranges, and yellows.

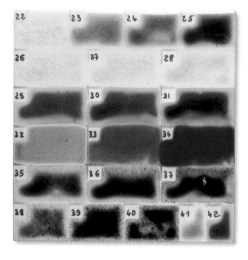
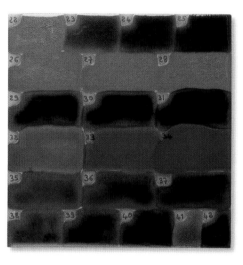

▲ Sample produced using a boron frit mixed with the six basic metallic oxides (copper, iron, cobalt, chromium, nickel, and manganese). In square 25, copper oxide and a boro-alkaline frit are blended, producing turquoise. The iron oxide has practically disappeared, which is common with boro-alkaline frits. These, too, are transparent glazes, and as such, the colors can be seen only when applied over slipped or white clays.

Alkaline Frits

Because of the solubility of most low-fire glaze ingredients, they are usually added to the glaze as frit. Their melting point is 1350°F to 1920°F (732°C to 1049°C). The fluxes in alkaline frits are primarily the three alkaline fluxes: sodium oxide, potassium oxide, and lithium oxide. Sodium carbonate is used to make alkaline glazes without frit.

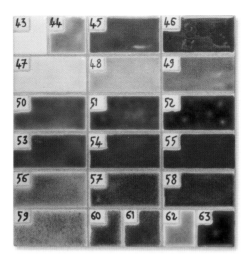 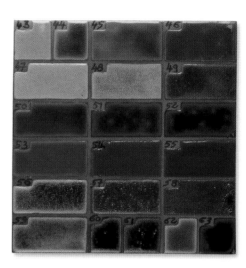

▲ These sample glazes, made with alkaline frit, are rather opaque. When applied to white tile, their colors appear lighter and more luminous; applied to terra-cotta tile, they are darker but still distinguishable.

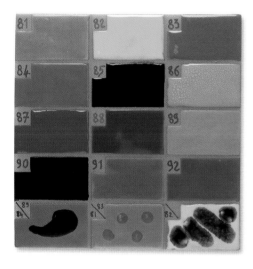

◄ An experiment involving alkaline frit with commercial stains, which tend to opacify. Applied to a terra-cotta tile, their colors are light and luminous. The result would be the same on a white tile.

▶ Alkaline frits can produce matte colors, which are well suited to low-fire clays. A high proportion of refractory materials needs to be added to an alkaline frit; for example, 15 to 20 percent of magnesium carbonate, zinc oxide, talc, titanium dioxide, or rutile; and smaller proportions (5 to 10 percent) of clay.

◄ The thickness of these glazes should be at least $^1/_{16}$ to $^1/_8$ inch (1.5 to 3 mm). A needle tool can be used to determine the thickness of a glaze when the glaze is wet.

▶ To experiment with various frits, blend 50 percent alkaline and 50 percent lead frit together, add 10 percent of the desired refractory material plus a small amount of stain; then glaze and fire a test tile. Proceed in the same manner with any frit; the possibilities are limitless.

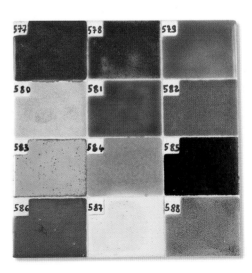

Stoneware Glazes

The method for preparing glazes for stoneware is complicated. One of the determining factors is the way in which they are applied. Their thickness varies between $1/16$ and $1/8$ inch (1.5 and 3 mm).

The ingredients are ground finely or bought in finely ground form; they are mixed in water and applied to bisque ware. The glazed work is usually fired to 2282°F to 2350°F (1250°C to 1288°C); this should cause the glaze to melt and become homogenous.

◄ This form by Carlets was enhanced with a glaze composed of mineral salts.

Alkaline or Basic Group:
Na_2O, K_2O, Li_2O

Neutral or Stabilizing Group:
Al_2O_3, B_2O_3

Acid or Glass-Forming Group:
SiO_2, TiO_2, ZrO_2, SnO_2

Alkaline Earth/Metals Group:
CaO, BaO, SrO, MgO, ZnO, PbO

"BASE 1" GLAZE RECIPE	
Feldspar	50%
Whiting	30%
Kaolín	10%
Silica	10%
Total	100%

◄ Thrown in two sections on the wheel, with glaze composed of rutile, iron oxide, and cobalt oxideo.

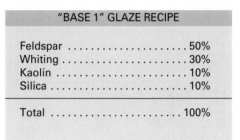

▲ These two samples use the Base 1 glaze recipe. The first, which is darker, is made according to the recipe referred to as Base 1 (100 g), to which 10 percent alumina, 10 percent zinc oxide, 0.2 percent cobalt oxide, and 1 percent iron oxide are added. The lighter sample contains the following additions to the 100 g of Base 1: 10 percent talc, 10 percent light rutile, and 0.25 percent cobalt oxide.

▲ The glaze on the left sample uses 100 g of the Base 1 recipe plus 10 percent dolomite and 0.25 percent chromium oxide. The glaze on the right contains 100 g of Base 1 recipe, plus 10 percent lithium carbonate, 10 percent titanium dioxide, and 5 percent of a light green commercial stain.

▲ The recipes for these three samples of Base 1 (100 g) with additions are as follows: the first (far left tile), 10 percent tin oxide, 10 percent barium carbonate, 0.3 percent chromium oxide; the second (2029), 10 percent magnesium carbonate, 10 percent tin oxide, 0.25 percent chromium oxide; and the third (2063), 10 percent lithium carbonate, 10 percent tin oxide, and 0.1 percent chromium oxide. All of these samples were fired to 2282°F (1250°C) in an electric kiln.

Values of Stoneware Recipes

Stoneware glazes are generally made up of clays, silica, feldspars, carbonates, and other components.

- **Clays:** white clays free of iron oxide, kaolin, and bentonite
- **Silica:** quartz
- **Feldspars:** sodium, potassium, and lithium feldspars, or nepheline syenite
- **Carbonates:** calcium carbonate, magnesium carbonate, dolomite, talc, barium carbonate, or strontium carbonate

RECIPES				
Material	Minimum%	Maximum%	Average %	Error%
Silica	0	30	12.2	13.1
Feldspar	60	85	72.2	11.1
Carbonates	10	15	12.5	2.9
Material	Minimum%	Maximum%	Average %	Error%
Clays	3	38	18.3	9.9
Sílica	5	35	19.8	9.2
Feldspatr	0	65	40.4	14.9
Carbonates	10	35	12.6	5.6

▲ The possibilities offered by stoneware glazes are infinite. You could spend a lifetime researching them and never run out of ideas.

Any of the above ranges of materials can be used to make a glaze for stoneware; they provide an average percentage for every material, and 10 to 20 percent of each of the materials mentioned on pages 88 to 95 can be added. The glaze is applied to a sample tile and fired to 2282°F (1250°C). This will produce very interesting glazes, and colorants can be added to achieve the desired tones. The properties of the raw ingredients will also be identifiable because those that contain a flux will appear glossy, those that contain refractory material will be matte, and the ingredients that contain an opacifier will appear opaque.

When experimenting, it's important to begin with a base recipe for a specific temperature; for example, the Base 1 recipe on the previous page, which is fired to 2282°F (1250°C). The additions are expressed as a percentage of weight.

▼ Maria Bofill, from the *Cups* series. Porcelain, with high-fire glazes

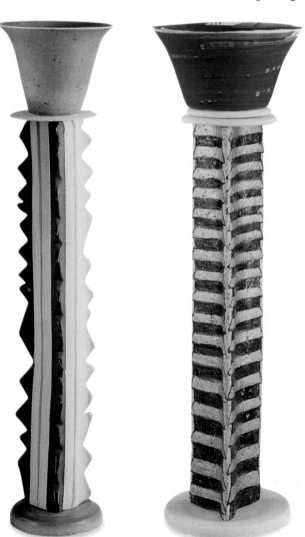

◀ Richard Manz, Wheel-thrown vessel. Pyritic stoneware, with a high-fire white glaze. The dark spots visible on the surface come from the pyritic clay.

Copper Reds

Copper red glazes are legendary and sought after by ceramists, perhaps because they are so difficult to produce and because they pose a challenge during every firing.

Copper oxide in a reduction atmosphere produces very fine colloidal particles of cuprous oxide, which help produce the characteristic red color. In the reduction process, copper is very susceptible to the changes in its chemical state, and it easily transforms in the reaction $2CuO + CO \text{ Æ } Cu_2O + CO_2$. A glaze that would be green in a neutral or oxidizing atmosphere changes to red in a reducing one. It's difficult to maintain an even reduction atmosphere throughout the kiln, so the color can range from blood red to pink.

In addition to the type of kiln and the use of reduction, the ingredients that make up copper red glazes are very important. All the recipes have a set of basic components in common, as specified in the following paragraphs:

Feldspars and nepheline syenite. These are the fluxes. Their percentage in the recipe varies from 26 to 75 percent.

Silica. This is essential, since it forms glass. It makes up 5 to 30 percent of the recipe.

Clay. Clay provides alumina, which is a refractory material. It should be used in small quantities. In the fired state, alumina contributes viscosity and keeps the glaze from becoming too runny. In the wet state, the clay suspends the glaze. It is added in quantities of 1 to 10 percent.

Sodium oxide, borax, or gerstley borate and its substitutes. To create copper reds, the glaze must be high alkaline, low alumina. They make up 5 to 20 percent of the glaze.

Calcium carbonate (whiting). This is a strong flux that has a moderate effect on color but produces strength in glazes. It is applied in amounts of 5 to 15 percent.

Barium oxide. This is a flux that has a strong effect on color. It gives more depth to the red. It is applied in amounts of 2 to 15 percent.

Tin Oxide. This is essential to the recipe because without it, the color red would be very difficult to produce. It is applied in very small quantities—0.8 to 3 percent.

Copper oxide or carbonate. This is the basic coloring compound that produces the red color. It is applied in very small quantities, preferably 0.3 to 2.5 percent of copper oxide or carbonate.

The glaze is applied in a relatively thick coat to produce a nice red, but not too thick a coat, or it will run.

▲ Before glazing important pieces, it's a good idea to experiment by doing a few sample firings so the recipe can be adjusted if necessary. The glaze results are best when applied to porcelain bodies.

▶ The copper red recipe for sample 3003 is made up of 50 g feldspar, 30 g whiting, 10 g kaolin, 10 g silica, 4 g borax, 3g tin oxide, 5 g barium carbonate, and 0.5 g copper carbonate. As the samples above demonstrate, red glazes tend to run.

◀ Firing of copper reds using the recipe in the caption above. For a successful firing, great care must be taken to maintain the reduction inside the kiln by adjusting the damper and monitoring the temperature rise.

▶ This color is produced by reduction firing a glaze that contains copper oxide and tin oxide.

▼ In the reduction process, it's important to control the color of the flame. If the flame has a bluish tint, the temperature in the kiln will continue rising. If it is red, it will decrease.

▲ In a reduction firing, there may be back pressure in the kiln, which will cause the flame to come out of the spy hole. If the flame is bluish, it indicates that there is an oxidizing atmosphere inside the kiln. A red flame indicates a strong reduction.

Reduction Firing Curve

The method of creating reduction depends on many factors, especially the kiln. It's preferable to use a downdraft gas kiln. An oxidation atmosphere is used before reaching the reduction range of 1550°F to 1850°F (843°C to 1010°C). When the firing gets to this temperature range, the damper should be partially closed so the flame comes out the spy hole; use the pyrometer on the kiln to check that the temperature continues to rise. When the temperature peaks, generally at 2350°F (1288°C), a strong reduction is created by closing off the air to the burners and opening the damper slightly, but not entirely. This will put the kiln into strong reduction, and the temperature will drop; this doesn't matter because the kiln needs to cool during this reduction soak. Then the gas pressure is reduced and the chimney closed off very slowly, without allowing the fire to come out of the burners. After several hours, the temperature should drop to around 1652°F to 1832°F (900°C to 1000°C). At this point, the burner holes are plugged and the chimney is closed off to make sure no air gets inside the kiln until it has cooled completely.

In summary:

$$Fuel + oxygen = oxidation$$
$$C + O_2 \rightarrow heat + CO_2$$

$$Fuel - oxygen = reduction$$
$$C + elimination\ of\ O_2 \rightarrow heat + CO + C\ (black\ smoke)$$

Reduction Firing Curve

Temperatura (°F/°C)

Close chimney 35 %

Close chimney 75 - 80 %; strong reduction
Strong reduction

Glaze vitrification process and start of reduction

Quartz inversion process

Hours

Ash Glazes

▲ The ashes are washed to purify them and to eliminate the remaining carbon and unburned pieces of wood; at the same time, the soluble materials are dissolved.

▶ Ashes can also be prepared by sieving. Sieved ash can be problematic because some of the soluble materials remain and can make the glaze react differently. On the other hand, when mixed with a flux such as feldspar, they can work just as well as washed ashes.

Natural ash glazes are a good choice for glazing containers intended for food. They are completely natural, and there is no danger of toxicity. They are also economical. Ash glazes are high-fired glazes applied to stoneware or porcelain.

The ash is a flux and may form a glaze by itself when combined with the silica and alumina in the clay body. Its chemical composition varies depending on the plant type and the part of the plant used to make the ashes.

Ashes are classified into three types: basic, acid, and mixed.

Basic ashes contain a high proportion of fluxes, such as sodium oxide, potassium oxide, or calcium oxide.

Acid ashes are made up primarily of silica, alumina, or magnesium oxide. These tend to be refractory, and their firing range is higher.

Mixed ashes contain moderate quantities of ingredients from both the basic and acid ash categories.

Preparation

It's important to know from which material the ashes were prepared (types of wood, straw, grass, seaweed, etc.); where they were grown; when they were harvested; and the content of the burned substances. The last depends on the amount of silica the plants contained; in thick trunks, for example, there is less silica than in the branches, and that determines the melting temperature. This combination of factors is what makes it difficult to obtain two types of ash that are consistent.

A wood stove can be used to obtain ashes. First, clean it out very well. Collect the type of wood you want to use for the ash glaze. Remember that it takes a lot of wood to make a very small amount of ash. After the wood has burned and the ash is cold, collect the ash and prepare it for washing.

Mix the ash with plenty of water so the unburned particles float and can be separated out. Let the mixture sit overnight and pour off the water. Repeat this exercise three or four times until the ashes are thoroughly washed.

Ashes can also be sieved through a large-mesh screen to remove the organic matter.

▲ Test tiles with ash glazes. The first (far left) was done with ash from olive tree prunings; the second, ash from pine needles; the third, ash from holm oak trunk; and the fourth, ash from heather. All four melted, which indicates that they reached temperature, but something is missing, since the glazes did not adequately cover the surface.

▶ These samples were glazed with the same ash, but with the addition of feldspar; that is, 50 percent ash and 50 percent feldspar. The combination was successful.

Ash glazes can be worked out mathematically through a molecular system, although this is very long and complicated. Another way to identify the ashes is to dilute the washed or sieved ashes with water, then apply them to a test tile, and fire it to 2282°F (1250°C). After the firing, notice the color and effect of the ashes on the clay body.

These glazes can be produced using prunings from fruit trees, vines, grass cuttings, rice straw, and pine or cypress branches. It's no easy matter to locate balanced ashes, but they do exist. The best idea is to start with the following experiment:

Using these two recipes, you can begin to experiment. First, make a sample with the feldspar alone, then with the feldspar in combination with clay or kaolin. Next, add each of the prepared ashes to produce glossy or matte glazes, depending on whether the ashes contain flux or are refractory. To make opaque glazes, add 10 to 15 percent of opacifying materials, such as tin oxide, zirconium oxide, titanium dioxide, or light rutile; the latter will produce color. For other colors, use metallic oxides or commercial stains.

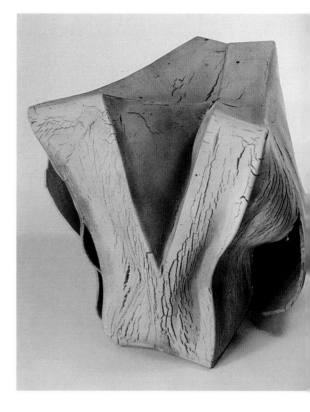

Feldspar	50 g
Ashes	50 g
or	
Feldspar	40 g
Ashes	40 g
White clay or kaolin	20 g

▶ Voula Gounela, *Metaplasis*. 31¹/₂ x 27¹/₂ x 31¹/₂ inches (80 x 70 x 80 cm). Stoneware, with porcelain slip and high-fire glaze

▶ Carlo Zauli, Textured sculpture. White, high-fire ash glaze. Ashes can be used to make all types of glazes.

▶ Ramon Fort, Bottle. The ashes were mixed with feldspar and about 20 percent talc to make the high-fire glaze on this form.

◀ Ramon Fort, Bottle. Ash glaze, fired in a reduction atmosphere

Raku

This technique is distinguished from conventional ceramics methods basically by its simplicity and the speed of the firing.

Raku is an Asian technique created around the tea ceremony, and it has been in use in Japan since the 16th century.

After glazes are applied to bisque-fired works, they are placed in the kiln, which has been preheated to 1472°F to 1652°F (800°C to 900°C).

The work is left in the kiln until the temperature reaches 1832°F (1000°C). At this point, the glowing pieces are taken out of the kiln with large metal tongs and put into a metal container (such as a trash can) filled with sawdust or dried grass. The container is sealed airtight to produce a strong reducing atmosphere, in which the colors and textures of each piece are created. After about 15 to 20 minutes, the pieces are removed from the container and put into water to set the glaze.

Clays

The stresses produced in this technique require clay bodies that are thermal-shock resistant. Clays that shouldn't be used are those without grog, or vitrified clays because they would crack when placed in a hot kiln.

There are different types of clay for raku on the market, but most white earthenware can be used simply by adding 40 to 50 percent medium grog.

Glazes

Raku glazes are fired at temperatures between 1652°F and 1832°F (900°C and 1000°C). The glazes normally used are boro-alkaline, with low melting points.

Before doing any serious work, it's a good idea to test a number of glazes, since frits vary according to manufacturer. These tests are used to develop the desired colors.

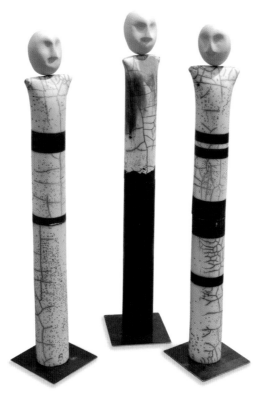

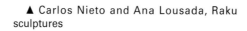

▲ Carlos Nieto and Ana Lousada, Raku sculptures

The following are recipes that will help with initial experiments.

GLOSSY TRANSPARENT	
Boro-alkaline frit	.70%
Silica	.30%

GLOSSY WHITE	
Boro-alkaline frit	.70%
Silica	.30%
Tin oxide	.5%–10%

METALLIC RED IN REDUCTION	
Boro-alkaline frit	.70%
Silica	.30%
Copper carbonate	.3%–3.5%
Tin oxide	.2%–3%

METALLIC BLACK IN REDUCTION	
Boro-alkaline frit	.70%
Nepheline syenite	.30%
Tin oxide	.5%
Copper carbonate	.4%
Cobalt oxide	.2%
Iron oxide	.4%

To achieve other colors, add oxides or colorants, as with any glaze.

◄ Carlos Nieto and Ana Lousada, Raku stones. Glossy, white, opaque glaze

► Josep Matés, Raku-fired forms

Kiln

A small combustion kiln (using gas, wood, or fuel oil) is a good choice. Today, some of the best kilns are gas fired—it is easier to create a reduction atmosphere in these.

In raku firing, it's interesting to note that at the end of the firing, at 1652°F to 1832°F (900°C to 1000°C), the pieces can be fired in a reducing to neutral atmosphere by closing the flue halfway. This produces more intense metallic reds, because by the time the metallic pieces are put in the straw, they have already had a period of reduction in the kiln.

▲ It's essential to know the colors of each glaze and how each will react with more or less reduction. It's possible to control the final result by testing some samples first.

▲ The pieces are placed in the kiln once it's hot. The lid of the kiln is lowered, and the kiln is fired until the temperature reaches about 1832°F (1000°C).

▶ Once the pieces have been fired, they are taken out one at a time with metal tongs.

▼ They are placed in a metal container of wood shavings or straw; the container is covered, and the reduction process begins.

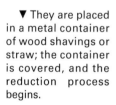

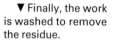

▼ Finally, the work is washed to remove the residue.

Paper Clay

Mixing paper of varying quality with clay bodies to reduce weight and open up the body is an ancient technique that has resurfaced in recent decades, thanks to ceramists who have used it to create new work.

This is an easy technique that makes it possible to use any type of clay, whether earthenware, stoneware, or porcelain. Perhaps the easiest step is selecting the paper—newsprint works best, but confetti, sheets of paper pulp, cellophane, and many other papers, preferably with no gloss, also work well. To use this process, start by shredding the paper into very small pieces and soaking it in water for 24 hours. A powerful mixer should be used to grind it up into a thick paste. Next, choose a powdered clay. If you can't get it in powdered form, let a block of clay dry out completely and crush it up before mixing in the paper.

The proportions are about 58 parts powdered or dry clay to 42 parts paper pulp.

To the wet paper pulp, add the dry clay, with no additional water. The water contained in the paper pulp will absorb and dissolve the clay. Once the clay is combined with the pulp, mix it again to produce a clay that's sufficiently plastic for working over cardboard, plaster, fabric, or any other type of support.

◀ Begin with shredded paper (newsprint in this example), and let it soak in water for 24 to 36 hours; the longer the better.

▼ A strong mixer is used to grind up the pulp and make it very fine. This is not a quick job; the paper takes a while to break down.

▼ Once the paper pulp is ready, add the powdered clay and continue mixing until it is a thick paste. Pour the mixture onto a surface that absorbs water.

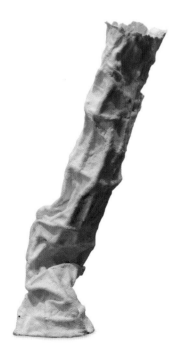

▲ Eileen Ng, Sculpture. Porcelain and paper clay mix. Paper clay can be used to make any form, but it is difficult to throw on the wheel.

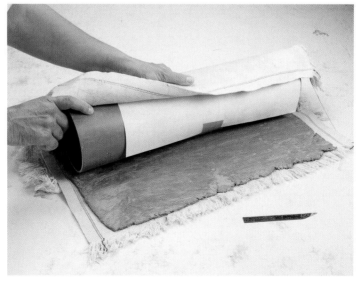

◀ The piece can be made once the clay becomes workable. The paper clay can be a very fragile mixture that requires some type of mold support—a plastic tube in this example.

Coloring Paper Clay

Metal salts soluble in water are commonly used for coloring paper-clay bodies. The salts are mixed in with the clay body, and as the water evaporates, it drags the salts to the surface. The effects depend on the manner and the speed at which the clay dries. The approximate proportions of salts are as follows:

- Iron sulfate, 10 to 15 percent
- Cobalt sulfate, 5 to 10 percent
- Potassium dichromate, 5 to 10 percent
- Potassium permanganate, 5 to 10 percent

These proportions are based on the dry weight of the clay, since the water evaporates

▶ Pedro Osuna, *Menina*. Paper clay, with metallic salts

in the kiln. Grog can be added to provide texture, but this makes the body coarser and thus more difficult to work. Metal salts are extremely toxic because they can be absorbed by the skin. Wear latex gloves when handling them.

Paper clay is frequently used by ceramists who wish to work on large porcelain forms and achieve translucence; for example, when making lamps or luminous sculptures. This technique makes it feasible to create pieces

that are very large but not very thick.

Another possibility is to use paper clay to fill cracks in pieces that have shrunk or to repair work that has broken. When the paper clay dries, it shrinks less, and the repairs are barely noticeable.

Once the work made from paper clay has been bisque fired, any type of glaze or decoration can be applied to the surface.

▲ This form by Eileen Ng is another example of the many possibilities of paper clay in creating a variety of shapes.

▲ When the clay body is mixed with the paper, it becomes very fragile, and it's very difficult to give it a stable shape. Cardboard, fabric, or pieces of wood should be used as molds. Corrugated cardboard was used as a mold for this piece. The color was produced with metallic salts.

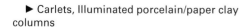

▶ Carlets, Illuminated porcelain/paper clay columns

Decorative
Techniques

The main purpose of decoration is to highlight the work in such a way that, together, form and decoration constitute a harmonious whole. Effective decoration must be based mainly on the clay and the glaze. Any other element is justified only to the extent that it highlights the essential values of the work.

Decoration offers an immense array of possibilities: the most commonly used techniques are slips, underglazes, resists, and glazes.

The following chapter will cover the most common and interesting techniques: slips, colored clay bodies, underglazes, textures, resists, and glazes. Still, the other techniques should be tried because confidence is gained through experimentation.

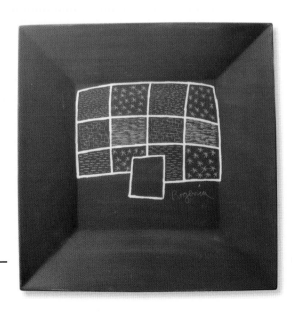

Slips

A slip is generally a liquid clay, which can be applied to a leather-hard or bisque-fired form. The application of white slip also helps brighten up the glazes. If applied to a leather-hard form, the slip must exhibit the same shrinkage as the clay body.

Just like clays, slips are plastic and somewhat refractory. They are basically made up of 60 to 70 percent ball clays or kaolin, 5 to 10 percent silica, and 10 to 30 percent feldspar.

The clays provide the plastic material, while the silica and feldspar are nonplastic.

Slip can be used on either single-fired forms or on work that is bisqued and later glaze fired. Single-fire slips are applied to leather-hard clay. In contrast, slips to be glaze fired are applied to dry or bisque-fired clays.

Leather-hard forms are generally dipped in a slip bath, but a brush or a sponge can also be used. It's not easy to apply a slip by spraying because the work is still damp and the slip doesn't adhere well.

The main method of applying slip to bisqueware is spraying; brushing and sponging are two alternatives. These slips mustn't be applied in a bath because a bisque-fired piece would absorb too much slip, and it would ultimately flake off.

One of the most important characteristics of slip is the presence of a flux in the recipe, such as a frit, feldspar, or calcium carbonate. The amount of flux will affect both the color and the gloss of the slip. In other words, the color of the slip is darker with greater proportions of flux; with smaller proportions, the colorants take on light or pastel shades.

When a thick application of slip is used (slip is even used to create relief), there may be some problems due to the shrinkage of the drying slip. To avoid this problem, the slip can be deflocculated. Using a large amount of commercial stains can increase the cracking. When slip is used to create relief, the shrinkage of the recipe can be controlled by adding 5 to 10 percent silica or feldspar to make it shrink less.

▲ For the most part, slip is applied to leather-hard work by dipping the piece in a bath. The thickness should be about $1/16$ to $1/8$ inch (1.5 to 3 mm).

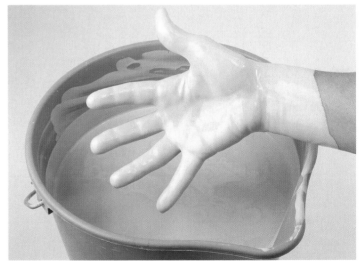

▲ When slip is applied with a brush, the slip needs to be fairly thick.

► Once the slip is thoroughly mixed by hand, the hand should be covered as if in a glove. If you can see through the slip, it's too thin.

When layering slips, the decorative effect produced by the use of two or more slips depends on the shape of the work, as well as on the color or contrast in textures between the covered and the uncovered areas. The possibilities increase when one slip is used over another, especially when using colored slips. If more than one color is used, the possibilities expand greatly. It's important to avoid creating too much thickness in the overlaid areas because excessively thick slips can flake off.

SINGLE-FIRE SLIPS		
	Recipe 1	Recipe 2
Ball clay	60%	70%
Kaolin	25%	15%
Feldspar	–	10%
Silica	15%	5%

BISQUE SLIPS				
	Recipe 1	Recipe 2	Recipe 3	Recipe 4
Ball clay	62%	20%	18%	25%
Kaolin	–	40%	18%	11%
Feldspar	36%	30%	18%	–
Whiting	2%	–	–	–
Silica	–	10%	18%	32%
Frit	–	–	28%	32%

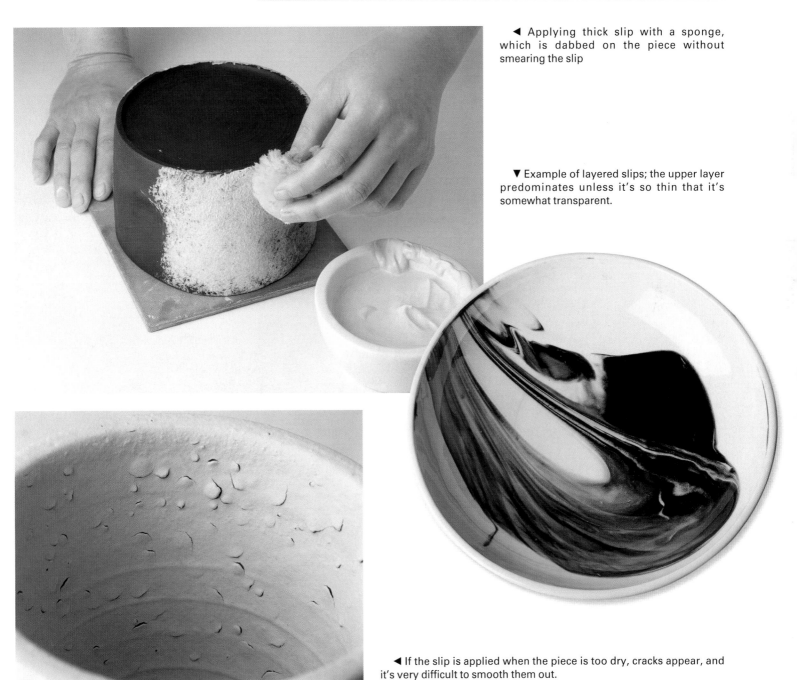

◄ Applying thick slip with a sponge, which is dabbed on the piece without smearing the slip

▼ Example of layered slips; the upper layer predominates unless it's so thin that it's somewhat transparent.

◄ If the slip is applied when the piece is too dry, cracks appear, and it's very difficult to smooth them out.

Applying Slip with a Bulb Syringe

The use of a rubber bulb syringe has become a very popular technique for applying slip. Some of the most interesting examples of traditional pottery were enhanced with slip trailing. Some contemporary ceramists also use a bulb syringe to apply glazes.

When using a bulb syringe, the slip must be considerably thicker than it is for dipping or spraying.

Long lines can be made by exerting regular, constant pressure on the bulb syringe. To make a dot, press just enough to make a single drop come out. The bulb should always be full—if air gets in as the slip comes out, the flow will be uneven and will produce blotches on the work.

▲ A bulb syringe can be used for slip trailing on a leather-hard form or on a bisqued piece that has already been coated with slip. When the bulb syringe is used to apply glaze, the work must be bisque fired.

▲ It's important that the bulb syringe be flexible so the pressure can be controlled as the slip is being applied. If the bulb can be disassembled, it's much easier to fill and clean. To make lines of varying thicknesses, nozzles of different sizes are needed.

◄ A bowl decorated with slip applied with a bulb syringe, then glazed with a frit containing about 0.25 percent cobalt oxide

Sgraffito

Sgraffito involves scratching the layer of slip with a sharp-edged tool to reveal the underlying surface and create decorative effects through the contrast between the clay and the glaze.

This technique offers two different approaches: scratching fine lines through one layer of slip, and scratching through multiple layers of colored slips. These possibilities don't need to be explained in detail because these techniques are self-explanatory.

It's important that the sgraffito be neat; this requires using a sharp-edged tool. If the edges of the line are rough, it's best to let the work dry and clean them up later with a brush.

Sgraffito includes many variations. One very effective method involves applying layers of various colored slips, then scratching through the layers to reveal the different colors, depending on the depth of the scratches.

▲ To create a design using sgraffito, first use a pencil to draw the design on the piece. Then use a sharp tool to scratch through the design to reveal the surface of the clay beneath.

▶ Pedro Gonzáles, Sculpture. Porcelain, with slips and sgraffito. The sgraffito technique can be used with any clay or slip.

To change the color of the clay body, whether because its original color is dull or because a particular decorative effect is desired, a commercial stain or oxide is added.

Finely ground commercial stains or oxides are mixed into the clay body. A lack of homogeneity between the clay body and the colorant may produce mottling once it's fired, even with very careful mixing. This may be due to imperfect grinding of some colorants. When preparing a colored clay body, then, the first thing to do is mix the colorants with a little water.

Adding Color

Colored clays tend to vitrify at lower temperatures than normal because many oxides also act as fluxes.

To color a clay, add oxides or commercial stains in the proportion required to achieve the desired shade. Keep in mind that commercial stains may reduce the plasticity of clay bodies.

There are two techniques that can be used to add an oxide or stain to a clay body. In the first, the colorants are weighed, the dry clay body is weighed, and then they are combined. This is the most practical method, especially if a specific result or a particular shade is desired. In the second technique, the stain or oxide is mixed with the clay body that is already moist; both are carefully weighed before mixing. This method is much simpler, but it doesn't guarantee a precise outcome because the amount of water contained in the clay body is variable. As a result, it can be used only when the final color is not crucial or when a color isn't being duplicated.

PERCENTAGE OF OXIDES IN A CLAY BODY	
Copper oxide	1%–3%
Cobalt oxide	0.25%–2%
Iron oxide	2%–5%
Manganese dioxide	1%–4%
Chromium oxide	1%–5%
COMMERCIAL STAINS	
Light stains	.5%–10%
Dark stains	.5%–30%

► The dry clay body is weighed before adding the colorant.

◄ The oxide or stain is weighed on the precision scales. Once the clay body and the colorants are mixed with water, they are blended uniformly with a mixer. The clay body is allowed to dry on a plaster bat until it can be wedged.

Trial Runs

If all of the clay will not be used for the first project, the remaining clay should be sealed with clear plastic so the color can be seen, and a label attached to the packet, with the name of the colorant and the amount used noted on it. Sealing the clay will prevent it from drying out.

Before creating any work with colored clay, it's a good idea to make a small slab of clay as a sample and apply various glazes to it, noting the characteristics of each one: shrinkage, color, plasticity, and so forth. Fire the slab and keep it for future reference regarding proportion, color, and glaze used.

◄ Maria Gelabert, Decorative bowl. Colored clays, hump mold, with metallic oxides

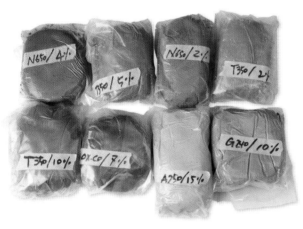

▲ Recently prepared colored clay bodies wrapped in plastic and labeled in preparation for use

▲ Before starting any project with a colored clay, make and fire a small slab to determine the final color.

▲ Colored clays offer many possibilities. They can even be wedged with other clays and thrown on the wheel or hand built.

► Samples of colored stoneware with various glazes. Fired samples make it possible to determine the final colors of future projects.

▼ Colored clay bodies provide an extraordinary number of possibilities in jewelry. These pieces by Natàlia Alaňá were made of a colored porcelain/white porcelain mix, then fired at high temperature.

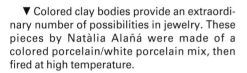

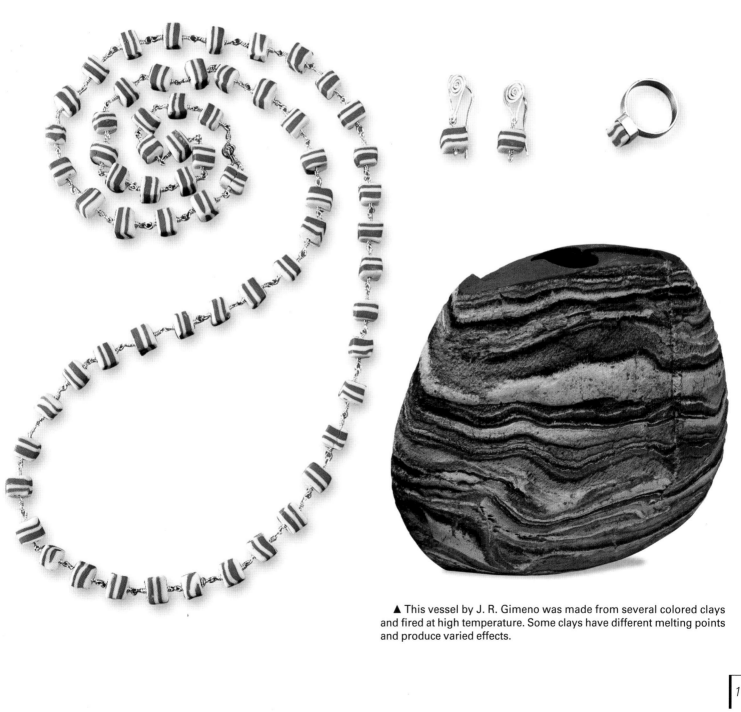

▲ This vessel by J. R. Gimeno was made from several colored clays and fired at high temperature. Some clays have different melting points and produce varied effects.

Underglazes

Underglazes are applied to the surface of a form before applying the glaze. To make underglazes, oxides and commercial stains are mixed with water, plus 20 percent frit. Underglazes are applied to bisque ware, and the work is generally low fired.

However, this technique can also be used at high temperatures, especially now with the new commercial, high-fire stains.

Application

The process of underglazing is at once simple and complex, and it's difficult to describe in a concise way. As with other mediums, the greatest freedom is achieved by decorating with a brush, since a brush obeys the movements of the hand and the intentions of the artist, who can work with greater or lesser speed, depending on experience.

Chalk and underglaze pencils can be used for more precise decorations, such as fine lines, spirals, and letters. Sponge application is a very quick and easy method. It is used as a complement to other decorations or to color the background of a piece. A piece of sponge is simply moistened with the chosen color and dabbed on the piece.

▲ Antònia Roig, Decorative form. Brushed underglazes using a very free stroke, fired at high temperature

▲ A sponge can be used to create decorations that can be completed with a brush.

▼ It can be helpful first to draw a symmetrical design in pencil on the work and then brush on the underglaze. A banding wheel works well with this technique because the piece can be turned quickly and smoothly.

▼ Chalk can be used to create very fine lines; its use allows a broad range of possibilities.

◄ Eulàlia Oliver, Wall hangings. With slip and underglazes, fired at high temperature

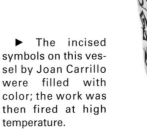

► The incised symbols on this vessel by Joan Carrillo were filled with color; the work was then fired at high temperature.

Resists

An artist often wants to protect an area of the work's surface before glazing for decorative effects. For this purpose, latex, wax resist, or adhesive templates, among other materials, can be used.

Latex is an emulsion that can be bought ready-to-use from ceramics suppliers. If the water-based latex is too thick, it can be thinned by adding a little water. Latex is brushed over an area on the work's surface to protect it from the subsequent glaze application. After the glaze has been applied and has sufficiently dried, the film of latex is removed. The background decoration is clearly defined. The resist area itself can then be decorated, or the work can be fired as is.

▲ Latex dries very quickly. After glazing the surface, remove the film almost immediately; then place the form in the kiln to be fired.

▲ Antònia Roig, Lidded vessel. Stoneware, with latex and glaze, fired to 2282°F (1250°C).

Wax Resist

Decorating with wax resist is a bit different. Wax can be used hot or cold, and the result is practically the same. However, the wax is left in place to melt off during the firing, so the resist area can't be manipulated or glazed before firing.

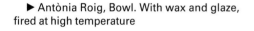

▶ Antònia Roig, Bowl. With wax and glaze, fired at high temperature

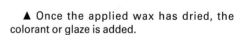

▲ Once the applied wax has dried, the colorant or glaze is added.

▶ This technique is frequently used for signs for street names, businesses, historical markers, and so forth.

his chapter offers six projects that are explained in great detail; they also provide further knowledge about ceramics in general. The purpose of this book is to give the reader some basic knowledge and ideas in a simple and enjoyable way, and to provide the motivation to experiment in the field of ceramics. We will focus on hand building with solid forms and slabs, throwing on the wheel at a more advanced level, and decorative techniques not addressed in previous chapters. I have attempted to cover as many techniques as possible within the space limitations of this book, but the projects presented barely constitute an introduction to the methods of working with ceramics. This art form has a common denominator among all ceramists: the possibilities are never exhausted. The more you practice and the more knowledge you have, the more there is to learn, research, and experiment with, for there is no end to the options of clay work.

Step by *Step*

Hollowing Out Solid Forms

*O*ne method of creating ceramic sculpture is to work from a solid shape. Basically, a block of solid clay is hollowed out, maintaining a uniform thickness in the walls.

The form should be hollowed out when the clay is leather hard. Large, solid sculptures should always be hollowed out; otherwise, there will be many problems in the firing. It's fairly easy to hollow out small pieces by starting at the bottom and maintaining a uniform thickness.

▲ **1.** First, make a drawing of the intended work. A rough sketch is all that is needed.

▲ **2.** Select the correct amount of clay, keeping in mind that if the form is large, sculptural clay should be used. In this example, the shape is very easy. The clay is struck with a wooden paddle to shape it; at the same time, the surface is enhanced by the cuts that are produced by striking it.

◄ **3.** To work with a large sculpture, the clay is cut into two or three parts in such a way that it's easy to put them back together. In this design, the sculpture is made up of four blocks. They will all be cut off at the same time to ensure that they match up; then they will each be worked separately. The cutting wire is used to separate the piece at the points least likely to ruin the shape.

▶ **4.** Once the blocks are separated, the top portion of the clay is cut off of the top of each (much like a lid). The block is then hollowed out, using a rounded trimming tool, until all the walls are about ¹/₄ to ¹/₂ inch (0.5 to 1.5 cm) thick. If the walls are thicker than this, they may crack during drying or firing.

◀ **5.** Before reassembling the two parts, use a tool (a fork works well) to score the surface; then apply slip where the two pieces will be attached.

▼ **6.** The pieces are attached with the aid of a wooden modeling tool, without disturbing the texture on the walls. The same process is repeated with the remaining clay blocks.

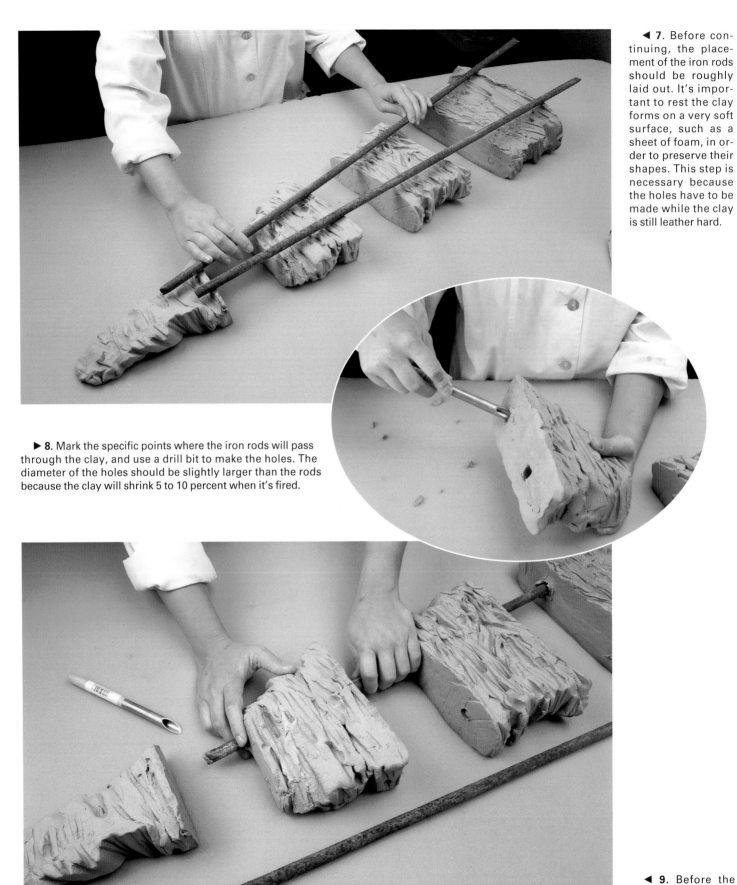

◄ **7.** Before continuing, the placement of the iron rods should be roughly laid out. It's important to rest the clay forms on a very soft surface, such as a sheet of foam, in order to preserve their shapes. This step is necessary because the holes have to be made while the clay is still leather hard.

► **8.** Mark the specific points where the iron rods will pass through the clay, and use a drill bit to make the holes. The diameter of the holes should be slightly larger than the rods because the clay will shrink 5 to 10 percent when it's fired.

◄ **9.** Before the clay becomes too dry, insert the rods to make sure the angles are correct and the holes are large enough.

▲ **10.** When the clay is bone dry or almost dry, the forms are decorated. In this example, iron oxide and manganese dioxide diluted with water are brushed on the surface.

▲ **11.** Once the pieces are covered with the oxides, use a damp sponge to blot the surfaces and remove some of the color. The forms are dried before they are fired to 2282°F (1250°C) in an oxidizing atmosphere.

▶ **12.** This is a fairly simple technique, with interesting results. This wall hanging was created by Ivet Bazaco.

Slab Building, by Ivet Bazaco

*S*lab building is a good technique to use when making large sculptures. It's possible to make all kinds of work using the slab-building technique. Before preparing the slabs, a full-scale model can be made using cardboard and then taken apart to be used as templates for each side of the piece, as well as its base. Wedge the clay to produce a homogenous block that's not too moist and soft. The thickness of the slabs can be about $1/2$ inch (1.5 cm), depending on the size of the piece. Use thick slabs for large works and thinner ones for medium and small pieces.

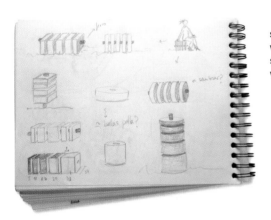

◄ **1**. Place the sketch in the studio where it can be seen while you're working.

▶ **2**. Stoneware will be used for this project. The slabs can be made with a slab roller, or two guide sticks and a rolling pin, then set aside for about two hours to stiffen up. Next, the walls of the work are drawn on stiff cardboard, which are cut out to make a template for each wall. Make sure the templates are accurate.

▼ **3**. When the slabs are leather hard, cut the walls to the dimensions indicated on the templates, maintaining the precise measurements.

▼ **4**. Cut the edges of the slabs at an angle with the aid of a wood strip. This angled cut is very useful when attaching the slabs to each other.

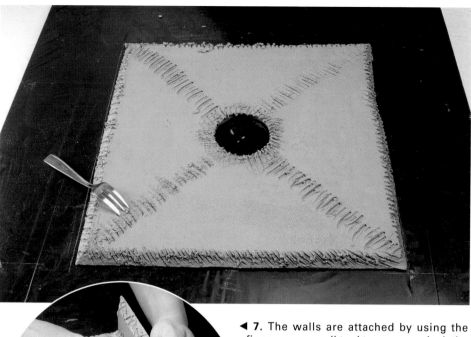

◄ 5. Use a fork to score the areas on the slab where the walls and braces will be attached. This improves the connections at the joints.

▼ 6. Brush slip on the scored areas, as well as on the additions to be attached. The braces serve as reinforcements, which will prevent the work from warping during construction and drying.

◄ 7. The walls are attached by using the fingers or a small tool to press or pinch the joined areas.

► 8. Next, the joints are reinforced by placing a thin coil along the inside angles; this is attached gently with the fingers or a modeling tool. The exterior is also pressed gently until adhesion is complete. When the clay dries, clean up the edges.

► 9. The process is repeated to install all the walls— exterior and interior. These steps must not be rushed; although they are not complicated, they require deliberateness.

► 10. A slab of clay is attached to every scored line. The slabs reinforce the piece and help to prevent subsequent distortion.

◄ 12. Before attaching the top slab, score and slip the areas that will be attached. The completed slabs should be handled very carefully and only when necessary so the areas where they are supported don't warp or crack later.

▲ 11. If the shape is entirely closed, drill holes to allow air to escape; this will prevent cracking during the drying or firing processes.

▲ 13. Once the top slab is scored and slipped, it is attached to the bottom section.

▲ 14. In work where the edges need to be sharp, use a flat rib to smooth them, with a wood strip as a guide. The form should be fairly dry when smoothing.

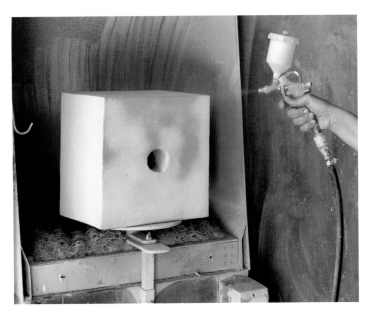

◄ 15. A spray gun can be used to apply glaze to each piece. Since this is a stoneware form, the sprayed glaze needs to be relatively thick.

► 16. Because of their large size, the forms are fired in an electric kiln in two separate firings.

► **17.** Once the forms are in place, the sculpture is assembled by running a metal tube through each piece, leaving a distance of about 4 inches (10 cm) between each pair of forms.

▼ **18.** The finished installation. The red to pink colors were created by a chrome/tin glaze fired in an electric oxidation atmosphere.

Throwing a Large Vessel in Two Sections, by Josep Matés

*T*he wheel is one of the main tools for ceramists. It can be used to produce pieces very quickly and therefore makes it possible to begin selling clay work within a short period of time. There are many varieties of wheels, but all have one common aspect: a round platform attached to a vertical axis on which the wheel head spins.

For a ceramist, the wheel can also be the main tool for creating large pieces—as large as the imagination allows. This step-by-step project will explore several techniques for making large work; the techniques are very basic and easy to execute. The artist Josep Matés demonstrates these techniques; he is well known for creating large forms on the wheel.

▼ Throwing in two sections is one method used to make the large earthenware jars that adorn many public and private gardens. There are a number of ways to make these pieces, including coil or slab building, but with these two techniques, only a part of the vessel can be made each day. The piece can be built up just 10 to 12 inches (25 to 30 cm) daily, since each segment must be allowed to harden before the next section is added.

Throwing the vessel in two sections on the wheel will be demonstrated in this project.

◀ 1. This technique may be the best one for producing thrown pieces with a large belly. First, place a wooden bat on the wheel head. Center about 20 pounds (10 kg) of clay on the bat to begin throwing one of the two parts the vessel requires.

◀ 2. The shape looks like a huge bowl. The walls of this piece are ³/4 inch (2 cm) thick. Make a channel along the rim where the second part will fit. Throw another bowl the same size and shape as the first on a different wheel or bat. The second bowl doesn't require a channel along the rim.

◄ **3.** When both bowls have stiffened up (especially the first one, since it will bear the weight), the two pieces are joined together, taking care to fit the top piece into the channel made in the lower half. The top half is still attached to the wooden bat, so the work can be handled without damaging it.

▼ **4.** Once the top section is centered and joined to the lower one, use a wire to cut the wooden bat from the clay and remove it from the piece.

► **5.** Mark the base of the top section to determine where the hole will be made to allow further throwing.

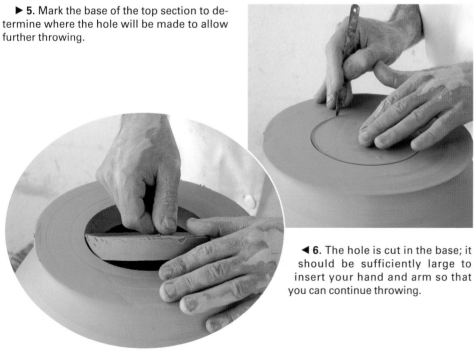

◄ **6.** The hole is cut in the base; it should be sufficiently large to insert your hand and arm so that you can continue throwing.

► **7.** The two sections are permanently attached. This is an easy process, since the channel previously formed in the edge of the bottom section can now be used to join the pieces.

▲ **8.** When the two pieces are properly joined, you can continue as if throwing a single piece, pulling up the extra clay toward the rim. When working on the wheel, always pull the extra clay upward; this is how the form is stretched. If the clay isn't pulled up, the form will be smaller and very heavy.

▲ **9.** The clay that has accumulated at the opening is pulled up and thinned to prevent the piece from collapsing. If the weight of the upper part is considerable and the lower part has thin or very damp walls, the work may collapse.

▲ **10.** Once the clay has been pulled up around the opening, the process is similar to throwing a single piece—continue thinning and pulling the clay upward. This is how the size of the work is increased.

▶ **11.** These exercises help give the work its final shape. The second pull is used to thin the work.

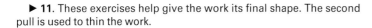

◄ **12.** When the work has been pulled properly, the final shape can be determined. Press from the inside of the form toward the outside with one hand while yielding to the desired shape with the outside hand. This pressure is exerted very gently, in perfect coordination with the outside hand. Both hands must work together.

► **13.** The artist preserves the round shape and has enough clay to finish the rim. However, in this exercise, a different method for finishing off the opening is demonstrated. Sometimes, a third section may be added to the work. Before starting the following step, the piece needs to harden, although it will still be fairly moist when the third section is attached.

► **14.** Throw a funnel-shaped form on another wheel; it doesn't need to be very large, but it should be about ³/4 inch (2 cm) larger in diameter than the opening of the main vessel.

▼ **15.** Cut the funnel shape from the wheel and invert it over the opening of the large vessel. The funnel is now in place.

▼ **16.** Center the clay as if working off the hump, and attach it to the vessel. This technique solves the problems that can arise when pulling the collar from the existing clay.

▼ **17.** Center the clay as if working off the hump, and attach it to the vessel. This technique solves the problems that can arise when pulling the collar from the existing clay.

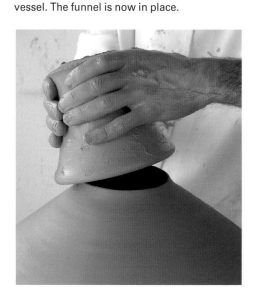

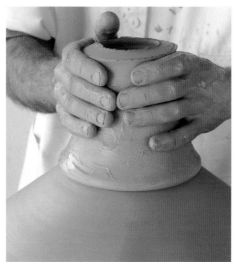

▶ **18.** The following step determines the final shape while the clay is still being pulled up. This technique allows the desired shape of the collar to be made. If the profile is not correct, the addition can be cut off and a new one attached.

▶▶ **19.** It's important that the joints not be visible on the exterior. To finalize the shape, press very slowly with the inside hand and smooth the exterior with a rib.

▼ **20.** When the shape is finished, use a chamois to smooth the lip.

▶ **21.** When the vessel is leather hard, the base is trimmed. Use a clay chuck or have one made of plaster that fits the wheel head. When making a series of pieces, it's a good idea to have the chuck ready in advance. If it's made of plaster, it will never lose its shape, even if the work being trimmed is heavy. The piece is carefully placed upside down on the chuck to trim the foot.

◄ **22.** The piece is centered and the foot is trimmed. Excess clay is removed from the base, which makes the piece lighter. It's now ready for glazing and firing.

▶ **23.** The finished vessel. A low-temperature rutile glaze was applied to the surface before firing.

Making a Large Oval Vessel with Salts, by Carlets

Two techniques will be presented in this section. The first will be an alternative method for making objects in two parts, and is designed for people who have not mastered working on the wheel. Also presented is a very interesting decorative technique for large pieces: incorporating mineral salts in glazes. This decorative technique was experimented with extensively by Carlets, who will present a basic method of decorating pieces on which glazes don't work well.

Slips with Mineral Salts

Slip is a liquid clay. In this project, slip will be mixed with mineral salts. In simple terms, adding salts to a slip involves adding a flux. When this slip is fired, it melts more easily and adheres well to the piece.

The salt that Carlets commonly uses for vitrifying slip is sodium carbonate. He adds it in a proportion of about 20 to 30 percent salt for each 100 g of slip.

The work is brushed with this mixture, covering the surface completely so that it is white. The surface is then coated with equal parts cobalt sulfate and iron sulfate powder. Because the slip is still wet, the salts dissolve and produce spots that can be light or dark and very interesting. When this technique is used on small pieces, they can be burnished before they dry completely. Burnishing is a technique in which the surface of the form is polished with a very fine tool (a smooth metal rib, a spoon, etc.), until the surface is totally smooth and takes on a satin appearance, as if it had been glazed.

These pieces are fired at low temperature, around 1760°F (960°C). At a high temperature, the salts would volatilize, changing the final appearance of the piece, so it's worthwhile to experiment with firing ranges.

Art often involves achieving harmony between the artist's conviction and his or her emotional intent in order to create a work that both the artist and viewers will appreciate. This depends in large part on reflection by the artist.

The designs used to guide the creative and production processes must be well structured. Few people are born with enough artistic talent to create without having to reflect and design; fortunately, however, these skills can be learned and developed.

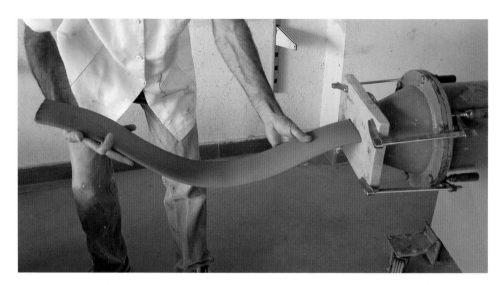

▲ **1.** First, make several slabs 4 to 5 inches (10 to 12 cm) wide and about 1/2 to 3/4 inch (1.5 to 2 cm) thick. This can be done easily with a pug mill or a slab roller; if these tools are not available, a roller and wood strips can be used.

◄ **2.** Throw a large bowl with a channel along the rim, and carefully attach the slabs. (See page 128.)

► **3.** Remove any excess clay where the slabs are attached. A buildup of clay can cause the piece to move off center. Use care when making these pieces; they can easily distort.

◄ **4.** To ensure uniform thickness. the excess clay is compressed or removed from the joint when the slab is attached.

► **5.** Slip is used to help attach the slab to the bowl. When joining the two, the walls of the channel help ensure uniform thickness at the joints.

▼ **6.** Once the slab is securely attached, the form is thrown and pulled up about 8 inches (20 cm). Only one slab can be added each day because each slab must dry before the next one is added.

▲ **7.** Once the main section of the form is complete, the collar can be formed. If there is enough clay, use that to finish the collar; if not, add it as a separate piece.

▲ **8.** Finish off the form by smoothing the surface with a rib to give it a rounded, closed shape. The air inside the form supports the shape; thus, the form can be rounded without collapsing it.

▲ **9.** If this is a completely closed piece, a hole must be made to let the air out. Wait until the piece is leather hard; otherwise, it will collapse after throwing. And if the hole isn't made, the piece will crack before drying completely.

▲ **10.** While the vessel is setting up, the white slip can be prepared. (The recipe in the chapter on slips can be used.) The slip should be weighed. Add 20 to 30 percent sodium carbonate.

▲ **11.** The salts should be weighed as well (equal parts of cobalt sulfate and iron sulfate), without mixing them with water. They are applied immediately, while the slip is still wet. Use caution; mineral salts are toxic.

◄ **12.** The slip is applied when the clay is leather hard. This can be done on the moving wheel, using a sash brush to apply the slip until the surface is covered entirely.

▼ **13.** Apply two or three coats of slip until the original surface is no longer visible. It's important for the first layer of slip to be thick because the salts will not adhere properly to a thin layer.

▼ **14.** Next, the previously prepared salts (equal parts cobalt sulfate and iron sulfate) are applied without mixing with water.

▲ **15.** The salts are applied with a brush, as was the slip. Push down on the brush to allow the salts to adhere to the slip; otherwise, the salts might loosen and fall off.

► **16.** Repeat this application two more times, without overdoing it. Once the shape is completely decorated, it must dry.

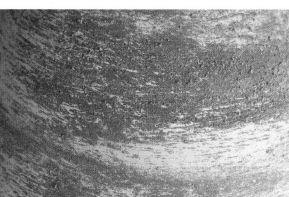

◀ **17.** As the slip and salts dry, they change color and become more intense and interesting. The fascinating aspect of this technique is the variety of colors it produces.

▶ **18.** The fired vessel is spectacular. The shades run from blues to browns, including ochres, cream, and burnt colors.

Coil-Building, by Yukiko Murata

This project presents a multifunctional piece made by the Japanese artist Yukiko Murata. She has lived in Europe for years, and her skill has distinguished her as a fine artist. Her way of working is very beautiful, and her work indicates a constant search for advancement. It is very creative in its expression, and it shows its origins in its very Asian shapes. She also adds a variety of materials to the forms, such as glass, gold, and porcelain. She is very tenacious in her creative goals, and almost nothing is beyond her capabilities. There are many ideas demonstrated in this next project; most are very simple and easy to implement.

Techniques

This project demonstrates various techniques; one of which is the use of crackle glazes. Most of the crazing can be produced by an increase in the proportion of alkaline oxides. Crazing commonly appears when it's not wanted, but it can be avoided by increasing the amount of silica in the glaze. On the other hand, crazing can be encouraged by increasing the amount of alkaline materials, especially sodium oxide and potassium oxide.

Since crazing is closely related to the contraction of the clay body, the problem may be avoided by changing clays. To ensure that the clay and glaze have the same contraction rate, material such as silica or grog can be added to the clay.

However, if a crackle glaze with black lines is desired, the fired piece is dipped in India ink for about 10 minutes and then cleaned.

This decorative effect is not appropriate for functional pottery.

Working with high-fire slips (a technique presented in previous chapters) and midrange glazes is another decorative technique.

The slip can be made from the stoneware or porcelain clay body that is normally used to make the work itself. The clay body can be altered to act as a semivitreous colored slip by mixing in the oxide or stain and a flux and bringing the slip to the appropriate consistency for working. Using the same clay for the slip and the clay body means that they have the same shrinkage rate. Thus, when the clay is applied as a slip, it will fit well and appear somewhat glossy.

◄ **1.** Yukiko always has a notebook and a pencil with her. Whenever she thinks of a design, she can draw it and later create it from clay. This allows her to work with greater precision.

◄ **2.** She notes all the details and the contemplated shapes in the book, using existing items as models. This precise organization helps her avoid errors and saves time.

▶ **3.** The forms are first created with stoneware. In this case, the base is thrown on the wheel because throwing is quick. Coils could also be used from the start.

▲ **4.** While the clay is still somewhat soft, the base of the form is created. It would be difficult to finish it entirely on the wheel, since the desired shape can't be made by throwing.

▲ **5.** Once the piece has stiffened up, coils are added. The coil-building technique helps solve many forming issues that can't be addressed on the wheel.

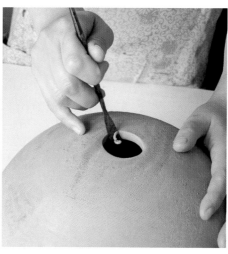

◀ **7.** Turn the bowl over and make a hole in the base.

▲ **6.** The bowl is polished and smoothed. To avoid knocking the piece accidentally, support it on a sheet of foam. This detail is very important, for many projects get broken by working with them on hard surfaces.

▶ **8.** Allow the piece to harden while the vitreous slip (which will subsequently cover the surface) is prepared. The slip used here is made of stoneware and porcelain clay body, to which about 20 percent borax and 20 percent black stain is added. The colorant is completely ground in the mortar and pestle.

▲ **9.** The stain is added to the slip to create a fairly thick blend. Using a sponge, apply the glaze without smearing it; otherwise, the surface won't be completely covered.

▲ **10.** After the piece has dried completely, it is bisque fired. The kiln is very small and was made according to the artist's instructions. It is a top-loading kiln and is also suitable for firing glassware.

▶ **11.** The bisque-fired form is easy to handle. Plug the hole in the bottom of the piece with a sponge to help contain the glaze that will be poured into the form.

▶ **12.** The interior of the work is glazed by pouring the glaze inside. The work is supported on foam.

◀ **13.** The form is rolled back and forth to glaze the entire surface of the interior, taking care to keep the outer surface clean.

▶ **14.** Once the interior is completely glazed, remove the sponge from the hole and pour out the extra liquid. The density of the glaze is difficult to estimate at first; it must be neither too thin nor too thick. Bisque-fired pieces absorb a large amount of glaze and can retain an excessive amount. If the glaze is too thin, it will not be absorbed well, and the interior will remain unglazed.

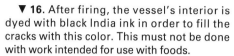
15. After the work is sponged with slip on the outside and glazed on the inside, it is fired to 2282°F (1250°C), the temperature that produces the final color. The interior glaze produced a crackle effect, just as the artist had foreseen. The ceramic piece may be fired as many times as deemed necessary. However, caution must be used.

16. After firing, the vessel's interior is dyed with black India ink in order to fill the cracks with this color. This must not be done with work intended for use with foods.

17. The interior is sponged clean after the India ink has been applied. Only the cracks remain black, and the effect is very attractive.

18. Here, the crackle glaze can be seen clearly. The decorative glass was added by the artist after the firing.

19. The form is not finished; it's still lacking the details that characterize the work of this artist. A small amount of frit with a low melting point is added to the area of the work where a small hole was made previously.

◄ **20.** A few sheets of gold leaf are prepared; these are handled carefully with wooden tweezers.

◄ **21.** A piece of gold leaf is cut and laid on the frit. The piece is fired again (without the decorative glass piece), this time between 1112°F and 1202°F (500°C and 650°C).

◄ **22.** After firing, this bowl can be used as a decorative object or as a plant container.

◄ **23.** Inverted over a water-filled glass jar, the vessel becomes an elegant container for plants.

► **24.** The gold detail gives this piece an Asian touch, which demonstrates the artist's creativity. This is Murata's definitive touch.

▲ There are many decorative possibilities. You can experiment by applying the crackle glaze to the exterior and the black slip to the interior.

► It can be highly satisfying to work with black and white, and to produce pleasing results with a touch of gold leaf. Murata often adds glass as a decorative complement to her projects.

Sculpting Vessels, by Barbaformosa

*T*his step-by-step project describes the making of two forms by Barbaformosa, a ceramist whose work is very interesting artistically for the creativity of her shapes. She puts all of her energy into making them. Her way of working clays is somewhat unique in the field of ceramics; she allows the natural imperfections of the clay to be enhanced by stretching the clay from the inside. This stretching produces striated cracks that give the piece a tremendous artistic quality. The inner surfaces are scraped and stretched to thin out the walls.

Barbaformosa is a contemporary artist of great spiritual and artistic strength. She can work with all types of clay; she works with stoneware, porcelain, and sculptural clays with equal ease. Once she makes up her mind to do something, limitations vanish.

One salient feature of this artist is her preference for the subtle or natural colors produced during the firing process. In her recent works, she uses very little glaze. She likes to work with clays that offer a great deal of contrast—black or white, gray or dark brown—for her intent is to enhance the natural qualities of the clays. For her, the most important consideration in firing is vitrifying the piece; however, as a ceramist, she appreciates and values the color that the fire contributes.

She customarily fires at high temperature in reduction atmospheres; that way, she can change the colors of the clays and produce anything from blacks to grays or dark browns, depending on the clay with which she is working.

Once she considers a piece finished, she checks the exterior. If she sees that the cracks are too wide in an area and might open up, she tries to avoid touching them with her hands. (She never leaves her fingerprints on outer surfaces.) Instead, she takes advantage of the open cracks to add metal staples to hold them closed and to keep them from opening up, while simultaneously using the staples as decorative complements to the exterior.

Everyone sees ceramics from a personal viewpoint, individualizing its various aspects. Some place it solely within the framework of archaeology, and others view it purely as contemporary expression.

Project One: Nonfunctional Black Stoneware Form

◄ **1.** First, choose the clay for the work. In this example, black stoneware was selected. Frequently, the shape of the work is suggested by the block of clay used.

◄ **2.** When removing the plastic wrap that protects the clay, take care to avoid altering the creases made in the clay during shipping. Cut off the quantity of clay needed, based on the desired dimensions of the piece. For this project, the entire block is about the size required for the finished piece.

▼ **3.** After deciding on the size of the piece, the shaping begins. This piece is worked by thinning it out and compressing it with a thick, rounded wooden rod. Make a large hole in the clay by pushing on the top at a right angle to the base, making sure to leave adequate thickness. The force exerted produces very pronounced compression in the clay at the base, which remains fairly thick.

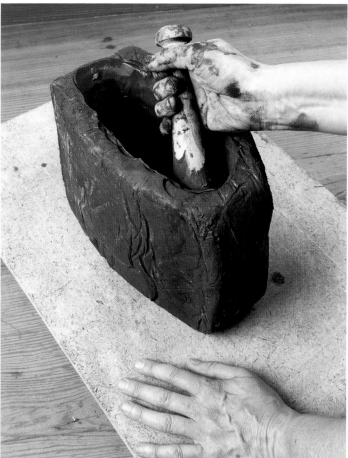

▲ **4.** At this stage, a pestle is used as a mallet to open a space by striking the clay from the inside, both upward and outward. The walls are thick at the beginning, but the piece is shaped by compressing the clay.

▲ **5.** The hand also plays an important role. The pads of the four fingers or the fist of the right hand is used to press the clay in different areas, deliberately causing cracks and irregularities as evidence of the process. At the same time, the shape is smoothed and opened up.

▶ **6.** As the shape gets larger, the walls are thinned with a rounded plastic rib. In some cases, the piece cracks excessively and a hole is formed. It can be fixed later in the process.

► **7.** Allow the piece to dry before any further work is done. Cover it thoroughly with newspaper stapled together to form a hood over the piece. This creates a moist atmosphere, which allows a uniform drying process. Sometimes newspaper works better than plastic because it's porous and allows air to pass through very slowly and the clay to dry more evenly. If the piece were covered airtight in plastic, the moisture would remain in the clay, and when it was worked the next day, it could collapse.

▲ **8.** The next day, continue working the shape from the inside, removing the excess clay in the base and the walls. Don't leave handprints on the outer walls.

▲ **9.** When the walls and the base are sufficiently thin, they are smoothed with ribs (these were made by the artist) that reach into all corners. The cracks on the exterior, which were caused by the compression of the clay, are left just as they are.

◄ 10. The cracks on the exterior walls produce some very interesting effects, which the artist accentuates by adding metal staples. These serve two functions: first, they keep the cracks from opening up further and causing the piece to break; second, the staples add a decorative feature to the work that gives a sober elegance.

► 11. When the work is thoroughly hardened, use a drill to make four holes, two in each end. After firing, they will hold two steel-cable handles, another external feature that will contribute to the finished work. The piece is allowed to dry completely before firing.

► 12. The work is completed with the addition of the metal handles.

Project Two: Nonfunctional Porcelain Form

◀ **1.** Porcelain can also be used, but it's significantly more difficult to work, and it requires great skill to make forms such as this one.

▶ **2.** Proceed as before (see pp.144 to 147), but keep in mind that there's a risk that the clay will sag. The clay has what is commonly called "memory," so when it dries, it reverts to its original shape.

▲ **3.** Using the pestle, the porcelain is smoothed and compressed, once again preserving the exterior cracks, since they are the most decorative feature.

▶ **4.** The result is a large shape with a very interesting exterior appearance that's produced by the cracks. But the process of making work like this doesn't end here: Depending on the resulting shape, the work can be continued on the wheel.

▲ 5. When the porcelain has stiffened up, the walls are thinned. In this example, trimming tools are used.

▶ 6. Next, several clay coils are made, as close to the same dimensions as possible.

▶ 7. Place the vessel on the wheel head, center it carefully, and score the rim. Moisten this area with a sponge dipped in slip.

▲ 8. Place the first coil on the form, and attach it to the rim of the piece, keeping the coil as round as possible.

▶ 9. Place the coils one on top of the other and pinch them together. Four or five coils can be added, depending on the dimensions of the form being worked.

▲ 10. Once the coils are attached, the form can be thrown on the wheel to increase its size.

▲ 11. When throwing pieces to which coils have been added, the lip commonly wobbles a bit; use a needle tool to trim it off and even it up.

◄ 12. The completed piece is ready for drying. When it's leather hard, drill the holes for the handles. This is also the time to carefully check the cracks and the holes, and if it looks like they may lead to significant breakage, add some metal staples.

▲ 13. The work was fired to a temperature of 2300°F (1260°C) and removed from the kiln. This is when the steel-cable handles are added.

◄ 14. The staples were inserted into the form before firing. Ceramists know that metal objects will melt when exposed to high temperatures. However, Barbaformosa has used wire made of kanthal, the metal alloy used to make the heating elements of the kiln. It's possible to install these staples and fire them in the clay without melting the metal.

▼ ► Much of Barbaformosa's work makes use of black and white. These finished pieces with additions are important contributions to contemporary ceramics.

Gallery

▲ Anima Roos, *Three Blue and Two White*, 2005. Porcelain

▲ Yuhki Tanaka, *My Constellation*. 22 x 22 x 20 inches (56 x 56 x 50 cm). Porcelain

▼ Anna Polo, *Petits somnis*. Porcelain with needles

▲ Tjok Dessauvage, *Return*. 10 x 8 inches (25.5 x 20.5 cm)

► Fernando Malo,
Spatial Landscape.
36 x 16 inches (92 x 41 cm).
Stoneware and porcelain,
glazes and stains, fired to
2282°F (1250°C)

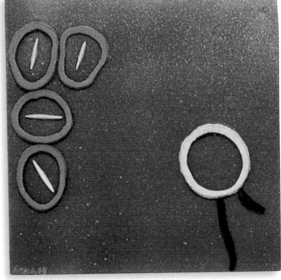

◄ Yasushi Inoue,
Changing. Various techniques

► Ángeles Casas, *Classified Container*, 2003.
8¹/₂ x 19 x 16¹/₂ inches (22 x 48 x 42 cm).
Stoneware with slips

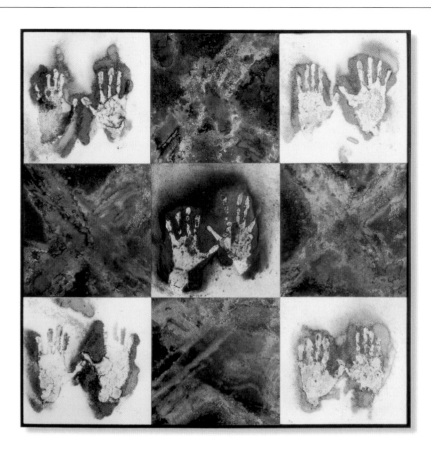

▲ Alberto Hernández, Untitled. 47 x 47 inches (120 x 120 cm). Clay and wood

◄ J. R. Gimeno, Untitled. Colored clay, fired to 2282(F (1250(C)

▼ Joan Serra, Untitled. Mixed media

▲ Carlos Izquierdo, 2004. 16 x 16 x 25¹/₂ inches (40 x 40 x 65 cm). Stoneware with slips

◄ Joan Carrillo, Untitled.
26 x 14¹/₂ x 6 inches (67 x 37 x 15 cm).
Copper matte glaze, raku fired

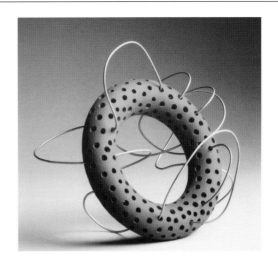

▶ Miguel Vázquez, Untitled.
Clay and wire

▶ Salvador Cortadellas, *Fountain*.
39 x 31¹/₂ inches (100 x 80 cm).
Sculptural clay, stoneware glazes,
fired to 2300°F (1260°C)

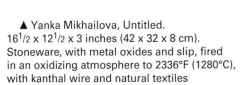

▲ Yanka Mikhailova, Untitled.
16¹/₂ x 12¹/₂ x 3 inches (42 x 32 x 8 cm).
Stoneware, with metal oxides and slip, fired
in an oxidizing atmosphere to 2336°F (1280°C),
with kanthal wire and natural textiles

▶ Teresa Gironès, Untitled.
25¹/₂ x 12 inches (65 x 30 cm).
Sculptural clay, slips, fired at high
temperature

◀ Rosa Amorós, Untitled. Round form, 6 x 19 inches; vases, 14$^1/_2$ x 10$^1/_2$ inches each (15 x 48 cm; 37 x 27 cm each). Sculptural clay, fired in reduction

▶ Carlets, from the *Balls* series. Diameter, 25$^1/_2$ inches (65 cm). With slips and salts

▲ Pedro del Río (Prioart), Untitled. Sculptural clay with high-temperature slips

◀ Juan Ezquerdo, Untitled. Mural, 59 x 39 inches (150 x 100 cm). Smoke fired

▲ Ángel Garraza, *Emblems*, 1997–1998. 52 x 57 x 21 inches (132 x 145 x 54 cm)

▲ Claudi Casanovas, from the *Minerals* series

◀ Maria Bofill, from the *Labyrinth* series. Diameter, 8 inches (20 cm)

◀ Dolors Bosch, *Cub amb escultura*. Sculptural clay with high-temperature glaze

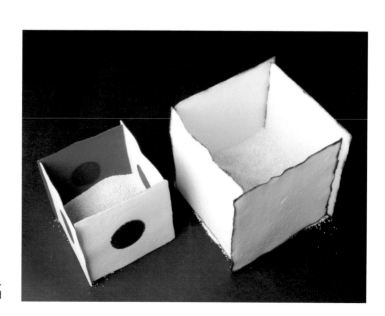

▶ Yukiko Murata, from the *Boxes* series. Porcelain and paper pulp blend

Glossary

a

Alkaline. A chemical term also used in the classification that Seger created for materials to calculate the formulation of glazes. The most important alkaline elements are sodium oxide, potassium oxide, and lithium oxide.

Atmosphere. A term used to refer to the environment created inside the kiln during firing. Atmospheres can be oxidizing, neutral, or reducing.

b

Bat. A clay or plaster form used to hold pieces on the wheel head

Bisque firing. The first firing of clays with no glaze

Bulb syringe. A rubber tool used for slip trailing

c

Calcareous. This adjective is applied to clays the main fluxing compound of which is calcium carbonate.

Casting. A method of making pieces in molds, using slip that subsequently solidifies

Chisel. Woodworking tool used to break molds apart

Clamp. A woodworker's tool with two extensions, one of which is movable. It is used to hold together the walls of molds.

Clay body. Commercially prepared clays

Cones. Pyramid-shaped objects made of a specially formulated ceramic material that melts at a specific temperature in relation to a specific temperature rise

Cordierite. A refractory material used to make kiln shelves

Crackle. Cracks produced in a glaze that result from the difference in expansion and contraction of the clay and the glaze

Curing period. The time plaster takes to harden

d

Deflocculants. Raw materials such as sodium carbonate and sodium silicate, which are used to keep clays in suspension

Double fire. A term applied to ceramics when they undergo two firings, the first a bisque firing, and the second, a firing with a glaze.

f

Filter press. Mechanical device that removes water from clay bodies

Firing stilts. Metal or porcelain supports used to hold glazed pieces during kiln firing at low temperature; they touch the pieces in the fewest possible locations and prevent them from adhering to the kiln shelves. Firing stilts are triangular and have three points—the only places where they touch the pieces.

Flux. A raw material that changes from a solid to a liquid in the firing process Generally, fluxes are used in glazes and clay bodies.

Frit. A specific blend of compounds that melt when heated. When they cool, they form a vitreous coating that is generally insoluble in water and impermeable to the gases in the kiln.

g

Grog. Ground, fired clay

j

Jiggering. A method of making plates and bowls by pressing the clay onto a mold fitted to the wheel, while a profile template produces the shape. The mold is placed on a wheel that turns during the process.

l

Leather (chamois). Used by ceramists for smoothing the edges of forms on the wheel
Leather hard. Semihard consistency of clays when they still retain some of their moisture

o

Opacifier. A raw material added to glazes to make them opaque. The most significant ones are tin oxide, zirconium silicate, and titanium dioxide.

p

Paper clay. A mixture of clay and shredded paper, dissolved in water
Plasticity. The capacity of clay to absorb water, to be formed without rupture or cracking, and to retain a shape
Pottery plaster. High-quality white plaster used in making molds

Pour hole. The top part of a mold that is used as a reservoir to fill the mold without completely deforming the piece
Press molds. Any mold—from simple, hand-packed ones to more complex industrial molds—into which the clay is pressed to create a shape

r

Raku. Ceramic technique of Japanese origin in which the pieces are fired for a short time and then placed in reducing materials to produce an interesting glaze
Refractory. The lack of a plastic quality and resistance to high temperatures
Release agent. Mold soap used to prevent clay from sticking to molds
Resists. Substances such as wax and latex that are used to protect areas of a form's surface from a glaze or slip
Rib. A shaping tool made of metal, rubber, wood, or plastic. Used when throwing on the wheel. Can also be made from a bisque-fired half-bowl or half-plate

s

Sgraffito. A decorative technique in which layers of slip are scratched away to reveal the clay surface underneath
Silica. Oxide of silicon that occurs naturally in multiple forms: quartz, rock, and sand. Size and purity vary.
Single fire. A term applied to ceramics when they undergo only one firing, with the glaze on the piece

Slip. Liquid clay that is used to join clay pieces together
Soluble. In ceramics, this term is applied to materials that dissolve in water, such as boron, sodium carbonate, and potassium carbonate.

t

Translucence. A characteristic of porcelain clay bodies. When the walls are very thin, they allow the passage of light, but not clear vision, through them.

w

White earthenware. Low-temperature white clay

Index, Bibliography and acknowledgments

Galindo Renal, Rafael, *Clays and Glazes*. Faenza Editrice Ibérica. Castellón de la Plana, Spain.

Gault, Rosette, *Paper Clay*. A & C Black Publishers, London.

Gault, Rosette, *Paper Clay for Ceramic Sculptors*. Neu Century Arts, Seattle, Washington.

Singer, F. and S.S., *Industrial Ceramics*.

Information gathered from courses at the Ceramics School of La Bisbal

To María Fernanda Canal for having had confidence in me once again

To Tomàs Ubach for his great support and help; without his patience and understanding, I couldn't have made it through to the end

To Joan Soto, my friend Joan. His professionalism is shown in the quality of his photographs. His good humor and precision in his work make him a great collaborator. Thanks for your patience, Joan.

To Ivet Bazaco, my great collaborator on this book. She's the one who made the pieces. She's also the one who put up with the nerves and the impatience firsthand.

To Josep Matés, another great collaborator, for his work on the large-format thrown pieces and for his contribution to the chapter on molds

To Carlets, for his great help and explanations of the entire topics of salt slips and paper clay

To all the friends who have stayed with me and put up with all the inconveniences and the time I had to devote to this book

To Antònia Roig, for opening the doors of her studio to me and giving me all kinds of help

To Isabel Barbaformosa, for having agreed to collaborate on one of the step-by-step exercises and for providing me with many pieces to use as illustrations

To Yukiko Murata, who has collaborated with me on another book; this time, she shows us her personal work in one of the step-by-step exercises.

To Emili Puigvert, for supplying me with all kinds of archival documentation

To Juan Francisco "Pancho" Martínez, for providing me with the works of many artists that were very helpful in illustrating the chapters of this book

To Elena Planella. for letting me photograph pieces from her exhibit

To Trayter Cast Clays for their availability and collaboration whenever needed

To Vila-Clara Ceramics, where the doors were always open to me

To Àngela Colls Ceramics Materials; I was always able to count on them.

To Ferrés Bosch Ceramics, for letting me photograph their exhibit

And to all the ceramists who let me photograph their work

To all the people who carry out administrative duties at the La Bisbal Ceramics School, for their collaboration throughout the production process

To all the ceramists who deserve coverage in these pages, but who could not be included due to space limitations